# The Milwaukee Bucket List

## 101 Real Milwaukee Adventures

BARBARA ALI

## ALSO BY BARBARA ALI

and available at:

www.amazon.com/author/barbaraali

*101 Things to Do in Milwaukee Parks; A guide to the green spaces in Milwaukee*

*Omar Meets the Sled Dogs*

*Omar's Hawaiian Adventure*

*Omar Goes to Japan*

*Omar's Apostle Islands Adventure*

*Omar's London Olympics Adventure*

*Omar's Arabian Desert Adventure*

*Omar's Caribbean Adventure*

*Omar's Cave Adventure*

*Omar Goes to the Renaissance Faire*

All photography is the original work of the author, Barbara Ali

ISBN: 1500858447
ISBN-13: 978-1500858445

# DEDICATION

To Libbie, who taught me that a messy house will always wait, but a sunny day and a great adventure are short-lived. This useful advice ensured that I have bloomed where I was planted time and time again, and have given me the best adventure buddies ever- my adult children, Melissa and Jake.

# THE LIST

# INTRODUCTION

The idea for this book began a couple years ago with a project I called, "50 things in 5 months to celebrate turning 50". It was basically a local bucket list. I had already been living in Milwaukee since 2004. I commuted for several years before that from Green Bay, when I was a member of the Air Force Reserve at the now defunct 440th Airlift Wing at General Mitchell Field. I thought I knew Milwaukee a bit, but I wanted to know it better. I had traveled all over the world to see beautiful museums and parks, but had not done that here in my own hometown. When I created that list I had three goals: better health, better relationships, and more fun. What a stellar summer I had sharing that project with friends and family! I got into neighborhoods I had never visited and met so many locals who were making a difference in Milwaukee. It encouraged me to keep on exploring.

When I created the adventures for this book, I used many of the same items from that original list. I also thought about what made Milwaukee special, and how it had changed from the city it once was. I scoured lists that others had already made to find great experiences. I studied Yelp, Tripadvisor, Facebook, Google and Urban Spoon as I read reviews about what others found interesting and fun. I had help from my kids who told me about places and adventures they thought should be on the list, so we have something for all ages. No one paid me or gave away services to be included in this book. In fact, most people were unaware I was writing about them until after I had checked them out. All the information came either directly from the websites for the businesses or just my own personal opinions. I haven't put anything in the book that I did not personally try. The people you see in the photos are those I met along the way. What I believe I've created here is a complete picture of our beloved Milwaukee. I hope you'll agree.

I have to give a shout out to my amazing next-door neighbor, Kari, who did the editing and helped me make this a better book. I'm blessed with good family and friends! They were good sports and went on many of the adventures with me to test them out (all in the name of good research!).

Anyone doing the **Milwaukee Bucket List** is bound to find something new and fun about our city. What I had not expected when having the adventures in the book was how they would expand my heart and mind. I hope you have the same experience, whether you've lived here all your life, are a new transplant to the city, or are a tourist trying to see what the locals do for fun in Milwaukee.

The list is not in any particular order. You can choose any item you find interesting. Then read below the headings for suggestions about where or how to accomplish it. This is definitely not a restaurant guide or all inclusive travel book, but it gives you a starting point with a number of choices that are sure to fit nearly everyone. I've tried to add some places and businesses that will likely not be well known to you. Some of the adventures might list places in your own neighborhood that you've already seen and done. If that's the case, I'd encourage you to choose a different location when you have choices. Get out of your comfort zone. I think you'll be surprised at what you might find. Some of these activities might be firsts for you, but don't let that stop you. Hopefully you'll find a new hobby or favorite hangout somewhere in the mix.

When I did the bucket list, I took photos and made a Shutterfly book to remind me of all the fun I had and the people I met. Maybe you want to do the same.

I've added some suggested itineraries by neighborhoods to help make it easier to find things in close proximity to each other. There are also suggestions for date nights, ladies/guys outings, kids, and even a fun list of things to do when your mother-in-law is visiting.

All information was current when this was published, but I've included phone numbers and websites so you can get the latest updates. I highly encourage you to invite friends and family for the experiences. It's so much more fun when you share!

# 1. GO BOWLING

Milwaukee used to be the Bowling Capitol of America. We don't hold that title anymore, but bowling is still a fun sport with a few nostalgic places to play the game.

**The Holler House.** Featuring the oldest two lanes in the USA, everything about this place screams vintage from the signage to the original wood floor laid in 1908. Women hang their autographed bras inside this tavern. Call ahead to be sure a pinsetter will be on hand. 2042 W. Lincoln Ave., Milwaukee 53215 (414) 647-9284

**Falcon Bowl.** With the second oldest lanes in the city, this bar with a bowling alley in the basement has been around for a long while. No frills. Good people and good drinks. 801 E. Clarke St., Milwaukee 53212 (414) 264-0680

**Koz's Mini Bowl.** For beginners or those who don't take bowling too seriously. There are only four lanes, and they are half the length of your standard lane. There's even a jukebox. It's in a casual bar. 2078 S. 7ᵗʰ St., Milwaukee 53204 (414) 383-0560 www.kozsminibowl.com

**Landmark Lanes.** Bowl where Kelly Clarkson, Gloria Steinem, and Everclear have all hurled gutter balls before you. 18 lanes and three bars, right next to the Oriental Theater. It has been remodeled but still has the old Milwaukee feel. 2220 N. Farwell Ave., Milwaukee 53202 (414) 278-8770 www.landmarklanes.com

**Bay View Bowl.** This is the alley that is most likely to remind you of the movie, "The Big Lebowski", because it has attitude. Glow bowling. Rocking jukebox and games. Automatic scoring that is super fast. It won't disappoint. 2416 S. Kinnickinnic Ave., Milwaukee 53207 (414) 483-0950

## 2. CHECK OUT A MARKET

Each Milwaukee market has its own character and charm. Held in parks, on streets, atop buildings, and even inside the Mitchell Park Domes during winter, there is surely something for everyone. You're bound to find fresh local products when you visit, as well as a few quirky surprises.

It's better to bring cash since the purchases are done directly with the growers and suppliers, though some do take credit cards. Bring your own bags to make it easier to carry your finds. You can find a complete listing, at Farm Fresh Atlas of Southeastern Wisconsin. www.farmfreshsewi.org

Here are a few I consider the best:

**Newaukee Night Market**. The newest market in town, this is a collaboration spawned by a creative group of people in conjunction with Newaukee. It started with a grant from Art Place America for "urban placemaking". They turned an unused space into one of the coolest places in town. One Wednesday a month, between July and October, vendors meet from 5-10 PM at a parking lot to sell the usual market fare like produce. Also included are a number of art vendors, performers, local music and a beer garden that supports local art organizations. Between 4th and 5th on Wisconsin Ave. www.newaukee.com

**South Shore Farmers Market**. Set in South Shore Park, this is my absolute favorite place to be on a Saturday morning in summer. Come for the crepes, live music, fresh produce, great views, and people watching. This place gives you a sense of community. 2900 South Shore Dr., Milwaukee 53207 www.southshorefarmersmarket.com

**CORE/ El Centro**. This Monday evening rooftop farmers market is a great place to get a view of the lake and Hoan Bridge. It's a green roof with herbs and greens growing in raised beds (above). This is atop the Clock Tower Shadow Building, one of the greenest buildings in the US. You can see what they are growing and purchase it! 130 W. Bruce St., Milwaukee 53204 www.core-elcentro.org

**Fondy Farmers Market.** One of the oldest markets in Milwaukee. All produce is grown within 50 miles. This market is a cultural feast from the veggies to the entertainment. Open multiple days during the week. It will surprise you! 2200 Fond Du Lac Ave., Milwaukee 53206 www.fondymarket.org/market

**Milwaukee County Winter Farmers Market.** Held inside the Mitchell Park Domes, this is a place you will love to visit during the colder months. There won't be much in the way of produce, but you will find local meats, honey, cheese, and all sorts of artisan goodies. Parking and admission are free. 524 South Layton Blvd., Milwaukee 53215 www.mcwfm.org

**Milwaukee Public Market.** "Fresh food. Local vendors" is a good motto for this place. Based on Seattle's public market, it features fresh bread, cheese, wine, prepared foods, flowers, and gifts. Open every day, it's a space that is very popular among the downtown working crowd and can be packed during the lunch hour. There is an outdoor market component during summer. Vendors are downstairs, while tables with ample seating are above on the second floor. 400 N. Water St., Milwaukee 53202 www.milwaukeepublicmarket.org

**Westown Farmer's Market at Zeidler Union Square**. June through late October, this Wednesday market is a great place to grab some lunch and get whatever you need for tonight's dinner. You'll find food trucks, live music, and plenty of fresh food choices from 60+ vendors. Don't miss seeing the Kettle Korn Cowboy for that real local flavor. 633 W. Wisconsin Ave. www.westown.org

# 3. ATTEND A LIVE PERFORMANCE IN AN AMAZING THEATER

Opera, ballet, musicals, drama, symphony…it's all here in Milwaukee. We attract big name performers, but we also have incredible talent living among us. Nearly any day of the week you can find something to watch in one of the many historic theaters. In my humble opinion, we have everything Broadway has to offer in terms of quality and selection, but at a lesser price.

Probably the best place to find out about locally produced events is to check out www.MKEstages.com. They call themselves "your simple guide to local theatre in Milwaukee…" You will find a listing by date of what's playing with links to the venue. They list more than 50 regional theatre companies including Milwaukee Repertory Theatre, Skylight Music Theatre, First Stage, Optimist Theatre, and Florentine Opera.

**The Milwaukee Theater** website lists all the biggest names and shows by type: top shows, musicals, family shows, stand-up, concerts, cirque, and dance. This includes the Pabst, Riverside, Uihlein Hall, Turner Hall, and Milwaukee Theatres, as well as the larger venues: UW Panther Arena and BMO Harris Pavilion. www.milwaukee-theatre.com

**Milwaukee Symphony**. For this widely acclaimed group of musicians who call Milwaukee home, go directly to their website www.mso.org

## 4. BECOME A SPY FOR THE DAY

Visit International Exports, Ltd., also called **The Safe House**. This popular spy themed restaurant and nightspot is good for some secretive fun. This can be a bit tricky to find if you don't know it's there. You need to find the nondescript door in a lackluster alleyway where you may be asked to give the password before you're allowed entry. What unsuspecting first time visitors may not know is that their every movement is being televised inside to already dining spies. This can be quite comical to watch as people who don't know the key phrase are put through the wringer! You might be asked to sing a song or do an incredible task. Each person must know the phrase. It's not enough for one person to vouch for the others.

Be sure to bring a quarter so you can exit via the secret passage found in the phone booth. Order your food and then look around the place. Read the walls. Check out the bathrooms. Peek through the peephole with a surprise. Look for other famous people who have visited before you. You're in good company! 779 N. Front St., Milwaukee 53202 (414) 271-2007 www.safe-house.com

## 5. SWING UNDER THE HOLTON
## STREET MARSUPIAL BRIDGE

This urban park is a project created by a local artist who decided to explore the space and conduct a social experiment. In the middle of a deep dark Milwaukee night, a group called Beintween put up swings using ropes and tires thus creating a pop-up park. Improvements have been made since then to increase safety and accessibility, but the main concept was a good one, and this has since become a popular gathering place for hanging out with friends.

The park features a dozen swings made from recycled tires, and even includes a couple of baby swings and a platform swing that will handle a wheelchair. The Milwaukee Bicycle Community shows movies here at summer bike-in movie nights.  No matter how old you are, you can have fun in this urban space. 1737 N. Water St., Milwaukee

## 6. TRY A BREWERY OR DISTILLERY TOUR

Milwaukee was once the brewery giant of the US. We no longer have the same brewers, but we still have several modern breweries and distilleries. They offer interesting tours where you can learn more about how their beverages are made, stored, packaged, and distributed. You will likely also hear a few tales about Milwaukee's history and get to taste what they make. For all tours, you must be 21 or be accompanied by a parent or guardian. The tours are informative even if you don't drink alcohol. Generally you can get a soda. For updated information all in one place, go to www.milwaukeebrewerytours.com

**Lakefront Brewery.** Started in 1987 by two brothers whose interest in beer began with a home brewing book given by one to the other as a birthday present. Their popularity and capacity continues to grow each year. Expect a quick and entertaining tour with a free glass and four beers. You'll hear more about how they acquired the current building from the city for a dollar (and a whole lot of back taxes). Be sure to look at the lights in the Palm Garden. They were designed to hang in the beer hall at the Plankinton Hotel, which due to Prohibition was never used as a beer hall. Lakefront bought them at an auction after the hotel was demolished. Rated one of the best tours in Milwaukee. 1872 Commerce St., Milwaukee 53212 (414) 372-8800 www.lakefrontbrewery.com

**Brenner Brewing Company.** The newest kid in town. Combination microbrewery and art studio, this place is so unique. Known for the 12-ounce beers, called ambassadors, they feature the artwork of a local artist and come with a soundtrack featuring the music of local Milwaukee bands. Your tour guide will likely be the brewmaster himself, Mike Brenner. He encourages you to come hang out, order food delivery from one of the many Mexican restaurants, and have a few beers. There's a large screen TV so it's a good space to see sporting events. Thursday-Sunday. 706 S 5th St., Milwaukee 53204 (414) 465-8469 www.brennerbrewing.com

**Best Place at the Historic Pabst Brewery.** More of a history tour about what happened here over the course of the brewery, this is sure to delight anyone who routinely does brewery tours just because it is so different. You will still get beer or soft drinks, but there isn't a processing facility to show. It's an exciting place to see as it goes through the renovation process. The gift shop is loaded with great stuff. 901 Juneau Ave., Milwaukee 53233 (414) 630-1609 www.bestplacemilwaukee.com

**Sprecher Brewery.** Not only do they do brewery tours, but also at Christmas and Easter, you can make an appointment with Santa or the Easter Bunny. They take your photo and turn it into a private label root beer, which makes a unique gift. This is a great kid friendly tour because they offer so many soft drink choices. Sprecher is known for using natural ingredients in their sodas like honey, vanilla, and natural fruit essence. 701 W. Glendale Ave., Milwaukee 53209 (414) 964-2739 www.sprecherbrewery.com

**Milwaukee Brewing Co.** This tour continues to receive the highest accolades on tripadvisor. People love the guides, the beer, and the tokens you receive to use at bars once you leave. Solar panels on the roof are used in the brewing process by heating the water for brewing. Growing Power uses the brewer's mounds of spent grain for compost. You'll learn more about their green brewing from the tour guide. 613 S. Second St., Milwaukee 53204 (414) 226-2337 www.milwaukeebrewingco.com

**Miller Coors.** First created by Miller founder, Frederick Miller, this is a historic building and grounds. You should enjoy seeing everything on the free tour, especially the unusual caves, which you won't see anywhere else. This is one of the longer tours and requires doing some steps. 4251 W. State St., Milwaukee 53208 (414) 931-BEER www.millercoors.com

**Great Lakes Distillery Tour.** This is a small batch distillery with award winning spirits. Everything is made using old world methods. The guides really know their stuff and are enthusiastic about what they do. 616 W. Virginia St., Milwaukee 53204 (414) 431-8683 www.greatlakesdistillery.com

**Central Standard Craft Distillery.** Just opened in 2014. They make white whiskey, gin, and vodka. Visit the tasting room and sleek bar, or schedule a tour. 613 S. 2nd St., Milwaukee 53204 (414) 455-8870 www.thecentralstandard.com

# 7. SPLURGE ON CUSTARD AND ICE CREAM

We've been called the "custard capital of the world"! Everyone who comes to Milwaukee should try custard, which is made with fresh cream and eggs. Most stands offer vanilla and chocolate, with rotating daily flavors added. Even Oprah encouraged **Kopps Custard** to start a mail order business of her favorite custard so she could give it as a gift. They still offer this service online. Select 10 flavors for your "somebody special" and they will arrive via UPS. Luckily, if you're here in the city, you can pick out your custard in person and eat it before it melts. They put out a monthly flavor forecast with a different flavor every day, but you can always get chocolate and vanilla. They have three locations: 7631 W. Layton Ave., Greenfield; 18880 W. Bluemound Rd., Brookfield; and 5373 N. Port Washington Rd., Glendale. www.kopps.com

**Northpoint Custard**. Great setting on the lake right next to Bradford Beach, but it's open only in summer. 2272 N. Lincoln Memorial Dr., Milwaukee 53202 (414) 727-4886. www.northpointcustard.com

**Leon's Frozen Custard**. A family owned business since 1942, they have a year round drive-in that some say inspired the Happy Days set. Vanilla, Chocolate, and Butter Pecan available daily, along with a special flavor that changes. 3131 S. 27th St., Milwaukee 53215 (414) 383-1784. www.leonsfrozencustard.us

**Gilles Frozen Custard.** Milwaukee's oldest fast food restaurant (1938). 7515 W. Bluemound Rd., Milwaukee 53213 (414) 453-4875. www.gillesfrozencustard.com

**Paleteria El Chavo.** If you hang out in the parks during summer, you're probably already familiar with the El Chavo ice cream carts that sell ridiculously fresh fruity pops for a low price. Now they have a new shop that sells the same icy treats, based on Mexican recipes, and made with fresh fruit from Pete's Fruit Market. You can also get ice cream in many forms- a cone, sundae, or topping waffles and crepes. 728 W. Mitchell St., Milwaukee 53204 (414) 755-2845

**Purple Door Ice Cream**. This is an ice cream store like your grandparents never imagined. Now an award winning destination for unusual grown-up flavors, you can drop in and treat your taste buds to something special. They use ingredients like green tea, herbs, beer, and absinthe. The above photo shows their ice cream flight featuring four flavors of your choosing. They are known to team up with local businesses to create new flavors and you will find Purple Door products on menus around town. 205 S. 2nd St., Milwaukee 53204 (414) 988-2521. www.purpledooricecream.com

**At Random.** If you're in the mood for ice cream cocktails, this is the place. You'll want to have your camera ready because everyone loves to photograph and post his or her cocktails on instagram. Listed on a website called, "World's Best Bars", they are just that unique. It's kind of dark with vintage décor. Cash only. It's a good idea to call ahead. Usually open weekends. 2501 S. Delaware Ave., Milwaukee 53207 (414) 481-8030

**Babe's Ice Cream & Desserts.** This is a popular spot for vegans looking to indulge. They always carry a few soy ice cream flavors and toppings. It's also trendy in spite of serving the Madison brand of Chocolate Shoppe Ice Cream. It maintains its unique charm. 2246 S. Kinnickinnic Ave., Milwaukee 53207 (414) 482-4000.

## 8. TAKE A DIP IN LAKE MICHIGAN

We have beaches all along Lake Michigan. Most are maintained by Milwaukee County Parks. You can check their website for weather, water quality, and beach conditions. Lifeguards are not on duty at all the beaches, so swim at your own risk. www.milwcountybeaches.org

**Atwater Park Beach**, Capitol at Lake Dr., Shorewood
**Bay View Beach**, 3120 S. Lake Dr.
**Bender Beach**, 4503 E. Ryan Rd., Oak Creek
**Bradford Beach**, 2400 N. Lincoln Memorial Dr.
**Grant Park Beach**, 100 S. Hawthorne Ave., South Milwaukee
**McKinley Beach**, 1750 N. Lincoln Memorial Drive
**South Shore Beach**, 2900 S. Superior
**Tietjen Beach/Doctor's Park Beach**, 1870 E. Fox Lane, Fox Point
**Klode Park**, 5900 N. Lake Dr., Whitefish Bay

The majority of people enjoy the beaches mid June through late August when weather is warmer, but there are some very hardy folks who take the plunge on New Year's Day, and we call them Polar Bears. If you want to join that elite group, show up around noon at Bradford Beach, on January 1, with towels, wool blankets, heating packs, sleeping bags, and a change of loose fitting clothes. Shuttles are available. 2400 N. Lincoln Memorial Dr. www.polarplungemilwaukee.com

# 9. CLIMB NORTHPOINT LIGHTHOUSE TOWER

The lighthouse at Lake Park is a historic, maritime treasure. It has a 74-foot tower with a stunning view of Lake Michigan, especially when there are no leaves on the trees. The house portion, which is Queen Anne style, was the former lighthouse keeper's quarters. It's now a museum with artifacts from former lighthouse keepers and the Great Lakes. It was an active lighthouse from 1855 until 1994. It's open for tours on weekends, and some additional days during summer, for a small admission fee.

The park is also worth a walk through. This is one of three parks in Milwaukee that was designed by Frederick Law Olmsted, known for his work in many other states including New York City's Central Park. Walk across the lion bridges. Rest on an Olmsted poet bench that is the same type still used at Central Park today. Find the former Nike missile tracking station, which is now a service building. Reflect on who might be buried at the prehistoric burial mound. Climb down the waterfall steps and pause for a photo on the gorgeous grand staircase. Learn more about the park at www.lakeparkfriends.org. You'll soon understand why this park is considered a Milwaukee gem. 2650 N. Wahl Ave., Milwaukee 53211 (414) 332-6754 www.northpointlighthouse.org

# 10. VISIT A FEW MILWAUKEE MUSEUMS

First off, you must spend a few hours at **Milwaukee Public Museum**. Take some time to walk the "Streets of Old Milwaukee", which are decorated according to season. It is festive with Christmas decorations and scary near Halloween. Peer into the shop windows. Look at the details inside each building. Then you might want to check out the fossil collection, learn about the Native Americans who live in Wisconsin, or try to find some of the typewriters in the vast collection. Many people don't know that Christopher Sholesis invented the typewriter in Milwaukee. Free admission to Milwaukee county residents the first Thursday of each month. 800 W. Wells St., Milwaukee 53233 www.mpm.edu

I've covered three museums in other places in this book-, Milwaukee Art Museum, Discovery World, and the Harley Davidson Museum. Some people don't realize that Milwaukee has quite a few smaller museums that can be done in an hour or less. With each one, you learn more about the history of the city and the people who used to live here.

**Milwaukee Museum Mile**. This includes five Milwaukee museums that offer a discount if you see more than one. Truth be told, they are a little more than a mile, but you could park at one and see them all in a day. Every May, this group promotes themselves by offering free or reduced admissions, but they aren't very expensive to begin with. You can see summaries of all the museums at their website, but they also have independent websites so I'll include both below. The first five are part of this program. www.milwaukeemuseummile.org

**Charles Allis Art Museum**. The former home of Charles and Sarah

Allis. This includes a world-class art collection, antiques, and changing exhibits featuring local artists. Go here for "movie time" when classic films from the 30s and 40s are shown by film historian, Dale Kuntz. He knows a lot about film history and you'll be impressed by the stories. 1801 N. Prospect Ave., Milwaukee 53202 (414) 278-8295. www.charlesallis.org

**Jewish Museum Milwaukee**. This museum preserves and presents the stories and history of the Jewish people who lived here in Milwaukee. They often host lectures or films. 1360 N. Prospect Ave., Milwaukee 53202 (414) 390-5730 www.jewishmuseummilwaukee.org

**North Point Lighthouse**. Maritime treasures and artifacts from former lighthouse keepers in a restored home and lighthouse. 2650 N. Wahl Ave., Milwaukee 53211 (414) 332-6754 www.northpointlighthouse.org

**Villa Terrace Decorative Arts Museum**. A lovely Renaissance style villa with grounds that drape over the bluff and take you to the lakefront. It's especially nice when the gardens are in bloom. You can go here for tea and coffee and enjoy live music on weekends. 2220 N. Terrace Ave., Milwaukee 53202 (414) 271-3656. www.villaterracemuseum.org

**Museum of Wisconsin Art at St. John's on the Lake**. This is a residential building which has a partnership with the Museum of Wisconsin Art, located in West Bend. They exhibit artwork from the main museum. There's a nice café in the lobby as well so come hungry. 1800 N. Prospect Ave., Milwaukee 53202 (414) 272-2022 www.wisconsinart.org

**Mitchell Gallery of Flight.** An aviation museum at General Mitchell airport, this highlights local people who played a role in the world of aviation, as well as military and commercial flight history. 5300 S. Howell Ave., Milwaukee 53207 (414) 747-4503 www.mitchellgallery.org

**Chudnow Museum of Yesteryear**. The newest addition to our local museums, it displays Avrum Chudnow's eclectic collection of early 20th Century Americana. It covers the history of Milwaukee between the two world wars. Set up with themes for each room, you'll find an ice cream parlor, apothecary, doctor, general store, etc. They host special historic events, which are always lots of fun. 839 N. 11th St., Milwaukee 53233 (414) 273-1680 www.chudnowmuseum.org

**Grohmann Museum.** Absolutely one of the best collections of European art outside of Europe. I marvel that Dr. Eckhart Grohmann was able to acquire such incredible pieces and feel fortunate that they are here in Milwaukee. The theme is "man at work" so every piece of artwork shows some type of profession through the years. This is part of the Milwaukee School of Engineering. You'll find paintings, beautiful stained glass, mosaic flooring, and sculptures. 1000 N. Broadway, Milwaukee 53202 (414) 277-2300www.msoe.edu/community/about-msoe/grohmann-museum/page/1311/grohmann-museum

**Betty Brinn Children's Museum**. Mainly an attraction for younger kids, this has lots of hands on exhibits. There are opportunities for role playing in the Home Town, which features kid sized local businesses: Harley Davidson, Sendiks Food Market, a TV studio, Waterstone Bank, a city bus and some changing businesses. 929 E. Wisconsin Ave., Milwaukee 53202 (414) 390-KIDS www.bbcmk.org

**Caterpillar Heritage Museum.** Learn more about the enormous mining machines built by Bucyrus and Caterpillar over the years. You can climb into the driver's seat of a simulator or explore the equipment interactively. There's an interesting display about the machinery used to dig the Panama Canal, and lots of models. 1970 10th Ave., South Milwaukee 53172 www.mining.cat.com/south-milwaukee-visitors-center

**Haggerty Museum of Art.** A teaching museum, with free admission, on Marquette University's campus. They have a diverse collection with exhibits changing eight times per year. 530 N 13th St., Milwaukee 53233 (414) 288-7290 www.marquette.edu/haggerty

**Milwaukee Fire Historical Society & Fire Museum.** This is one of five fire stations of this style built in 1927. It has the department's first ambulance, a 1947 Cadillac. See the bunkroom where the firefighters used to spend their 24-hour shifts. It's open the first Sunday of every month. 1615 W. Oklahoma Ave., Milwaukee 53215 (414) 286-5272 www.city.milwaukee.gov/MUSEUMHISTORICALSOCIETY.htm

**Hmong Museum.** See arts and artifacts displayed at the Hmong American Friendship Association, Inc. There is some beautiful needlework here, and a gift shop. 3824 W. Vliet St., Milwaukee 53208 (414) 344-6575 www.hmongamer.org

**Old South Side Settlement Museum.** A restored house featuring things as they were when the neighborhood was settled by Polish and then Hispanic residents. You have to call to arrange a tour or go during a day when they hold an open house. 707 W. Lincoln Ave., Milwaukee 53215 (414) 271-9417

## 11. SIT ON A HARLEY

The Harley Davidson museum is a must see for any motorcycle aficionado. This is the only one in the world. They also encourage bikers to bring their own bikes in for special occasions, so you feel a part of the whole HD experience. It's much more than just a museum.

The exhibits take you through the history of the motorcycle and its use across generations. Some of the exhibits are interactive. With more than 450 motorcycles, you're bound to see something you never imagined. There's a special kid area where children can put on the leather and rev their own mini motorcycle, read themed motorcycle books, and color. Big kids can sit in the saddle of the Harley outdoors and make some noise of their own. You'll also find an experience gallery indoors where you can sit on, touch, and photograph yourself and friends on the bike of your choice.

If you have the time, take a behind-the-scenes steel toe tour where you visit the museum and then go to the Pilgrim Road Powertrain operations facility.

The Motor Bar & Restaurant is open to the public, even if you don't have time for a museum tour. You'll find American fare with hearty portions. Be sure to check out the gift shop for a large selection of Harley Davidson themed apparel, key chains, artwork and more. 400 W. Canal St., Milwaukee 53201 (877) 436-8738 www.harley-davidson.com

# 12. HAVE AFTERNOON TEA IN STYLE

You are certain to feel elegant as you sip tea from the finest porcelain and eat finger sandwiches with your friends. If that isn't your cup of tea, so to speak, choose a more casual teahouse. Each tea experience is quite different, so pick one that suits you…or try all of them!

**Pfister Hotel**. Everything about the Pfister is elegant and grand. Be seated at low tables in front of the expansive windows of Blu, the hotel's stylish bar area on the 23rd floor. Take in the sights of Milwaukee below as a tea butler explains the local Milwaukee brand- Rishi teas. You select from a menu that includes scones, sweets, sandwiches, and cheeses. They even have a children's menu with choices that will delight the 12 and under crowd. This service is offered Friday-Sunday, November through March by reservation only. A secret tip- check out the view from the ladies room for a real treat! 424 E. Wisconsin Ave., Milwaukee 53202 (414) 935-5950 www.thepfisterhotel.com/afternoontea/

**Schuster Mansion**. Victorian High Tea with a different theme every month. You need to reserve a space in advance for the weekend-scheduled sessions. Additional teas are held during the week in December to celebrate the mansion decked out in Christmas decorations. They try to recreate the feeling and experience one would have had in the late 1800s. Feel free to dress for the occasion. You'll hear stories and history of the mansion while you relax. You can also get a tour of the mansion, which is still a functioning bed & breakfast. 3209 W. Wells St., Milwaukee 53208 (414) 342-3210 www.schustermansion.com

**Watts Tea Shop.** Open every day except Sunday, you can be seated in the upstairs tearoom above the George Watts china and crystal store. Afternoon tea service is from 11-4, though you can get breakfast and lunch here too. The menu for tea includes a selection of canapés, fruit, pastries, and a choice of gourmet tea. Kids also have an option that includes peanut butter and jelly. Be sure to save room for the sunshine cake (above)! Light and delicious, you won't soon forget it. 761 N. Jefferson St., Milwaukee 53202 (800) 747-9288 www.wattsteashop.com

**Rochambo Coffee & Tea House.** For a much more casual experience, drop in to this classic east side coffee house with more than 50 teas. Some of them are not offered other places in the city. 1317 E. Brady St., Milwaukee 53202 (414) 291-0095 www.rochambo.com

## 13. GET INSIDE MILLER PARK STADIUM

Whether you enjoy baseball or not, you should get a view of the inside of this amazing architectural space. Of course, I think everyone would love the whole baseball game experience from tailgating to hot dog vendors to shouting for the home team. And don't miss the 6th inning sausage race!

Miller Park features the only fan shaped convertible roof in the US, which can open and close in under 10 minutes. With expansive windows, natural grass still grows. It was one of Wisconsin's largest construction projects, built at a cost of $392 million, using $290 million of public funds, so it's really "the people's stadium".

With state of the art LED scoreboards, viewers get all the statistics for each player at bat, along with the speed of the ball as it is hit. You can also get views of the field and information about other games being played around the US.

Walk around the complex to see interactive displays and have your photo taken in a huge catcher's mitt. There are also restaurants that are open every day. If you have time, check out Helfaer field, a little league field in the shadow of the new stadium. Placed at the site of the old Milwaukee County Stadium playing field, it's a real life "Field of Dreams". Want to host your own family or organization ball game? You can rent the field for a few hundred dollars.

Take a basic tour of Miller Park from April through September for $10. This includes the dugout, luxury suites, clubhouse, press box and other behind the scenes attractions. If you want to put out the big bucks, for $100+, you can do Bernie's Slide experience with Bernie photo ops and up to five trips down the famous slide. 1 Brewers Way, Milwaukee 53214 (414) 902-4400 www.milwaukee.brewers.mlb.com

# 14. SEE ONE OF MILWAUKEE'S OTHER SPORTS TEAMS PLAY

Milwaukeeans are huge sports fans. When baseball season is over, it's time to head indoors to watch soccer, basketball, hockey, or even roller derby.

The **BMO Harris Bradley Center** is the only major, public assembly facility in the US with construction underwritten through the philanthropy of a single family. Funding was generously provided by the late Jane Bradley Pettit in honor of her father, Harry Lynde Bradley, co-founder of the Allen-Bradley Company, which is now Rockwell Automation. The Bradley Center takes up six acres of land and holds more than 150 events every year. This is the place to see the **Milwaukee Bucks**, **Milwaukee Admirals**, and the college team, **Marquette Golden Eagles**. You can buy tickets using Ticketmaster or at the box office. 1001 N. 4th St., Milwaukee 53203 (414) 227-0400 www.bmoharrisbradleycenter.com

The **UW-Milwaukee Panther Arena**, previously called US Cellular Arena, is where you'll find **The Milwaukee Wave** indoor soccer team, **UWM Panthers**, and **The Brewcity Bruisers** women's roller derby. The arena has 12,700 seats. Tickets are sold at the box office in the Milwaukee Theatre at 500 W. Kilbourn Ave. The arena is at 400 W. Kilbourn Ave., Milwaukee 53203 (800) 745-3000 www.uwmmilwaukeepantherarena.com

Just outside the Arena is the Wisconsin Athletic Hall of Fame, a promenade honoring 130 outstanding sports figures whose achievements earned them special acclaim. New members are inducted every two years. They come from a variety of sports. Take a walk. Who do you recognize?

## 15. GO INSIDE A BANK VAULT WITHOUT ROBBING A BANK

Milwaukee County Historical Society is a historic space with everything you ever wanted to know about Milwaukee's past, right at your fingertips. Their mission has been to collect, preserve, and make available materials relating to the city's history. A very small portion is on display at any one time. The building used to be a bank, and they have restored the building so that you can see the old bank vaults. There are six in all. Some are used for storage of artifacts. The bank was "robbed" by Johnny Depp, as John Dillinger, in the making of the 2009 film, "Public Enemies". The interior of the building is quite stunning with gilded marble columns, and classy chandeliers. The space is often rented out for weddings. The upper floor contains a small but power packed library of genealogical materials and reference books. You can do research here or just visit the museum for $5. 910 N. Old World Third St., Milwaukee 53203 (414) 273-8288 www.milwaukeehistory.net

# 16. BE ADVENTUROUS!
# TRY SOMETHING NEW!

This is a very personal choice, but I'll mention a few extraordinary opportunities available that I haven't mentioned in other parts of this book, and let you choose. The point is to break out of the doldrums to meet some new people, see some new things, and have a little fun.

**Meetup** is a great place to find groups meeting in Milwaukee that have something of interest to you. www.meetup.com and put in Milwaukee. Then browse the groups. When you find something you like, join them to find out about future meetups.

Check out other classes and ideas at your local park and recreation office or through **UWM School of Continuing Education.**

**Unicycle at Red Arrow Park**. The MSOE students offer free weekly lessons during warmer weather for anyone who wants to give this a try. Unicycles are provided and you get a certificate to prove you've done it. 920 N. Water St., Milwaukee 53202 www.facebook.com/msoeuniclub

**Kiteboard at Lake Michigan**. Take a lesson in kiteboarding or Kitesurfing with Adventure Bicycle & Kiteboarding. They launch at Bay View Park or Bradford Beach. Contact Kiteboard Milwaukee for information about lessons. (414) 520-1493 www.kiteboardmilwaukee.com

**Milwaukee Community Sailing Center**. Learn how to sail. There are courses for every age group. Become a member and you'll have free access to their fleet of 80 boats. 1450 N. Lincoln Memorial Dr., Milwaukee 53202 (414) 277-9094 www.sailingcenter.org

**Beach Volleyball.** Beach volleyball is a big deal in Milwaukee. Bradford Beach hosts tournaments and leagues during summer. Book a court with your friends. 2400 N. Lincoln Memorial Dr., Milwaukee 53211 (414) 967-9531 www.bradfordbeachjam.com

**Running Classes at Performance Running Outfitters.** Have you ever wondered if you could be a better runner? Or maybe you want to try your first marathon? They have classes that teach you how to have better form, help you get fit, and find the right shoes to get you started. Clinics are run through their Shorewood and Brookfield stores. www.performancerunning.com

**Remote Control Boats, Aircraft, Cars, and Trains.** Pick up a new hobby and find a club at Greenfield News & Hobby. 6815 W. Layton Ave., Greenfield 53220 (414) 281-1800 www.greenfieldhobby.com

**Drum Circles.** Come for a lesson series. Come back for Drum Circles. Workshops for all ages. Classes held at Rhythm for Unity in the Unity Enterprises Shoppe, 1325 N. 72$^{nd}$ St., Wauwatosa 53213 (414) 774-8848.www.rhythmforunity.com. Additional classes at Wisconsin Conservatory of Music, 1584 N. Prospect Ave., Milwaukee 53202 (414) 276-5760 www.wcmusic.org

**Ping Pong.** You can pay to play ping-pong at one of 12 high quality tables and dine at Evolution Gastro Pong. I'm sure Forrest Gump would have loved this place and you might too! 233 E. Chicago St., Milwaukee 53202 (414) 831-7746 www.evolution.mke.com

**Rock Climbing at Turner Hall.** Most people know Turner Hall as a concert venue, but few know there's a rock wall inside. They will teach you everything you need to know in a "learn to climb lesson". 1034 N. 4$^{th}$ St., Milwaukee 53203 (414) 272-1733 www.ascentgym.com

**Extreme Biking.** The Rock Sports Complex has a wide variety of adventure sports, both summer and winter. Maybe you want to rent a bike and try out the gravity trails, or take a few runs on the BMX track. It's all good! 7900 Crystal Ridge Rd., Franklin 53132 (414) 529-7676 www.mke.rockbikepark.com

**Pole Dancing.** Join a class in burlesque, pole, or chair dancing to get fit and have fun. Builds upper body strength. Adults only. Blush Pole Fitness & Dance. 7701 W. Greenfield Ave., West Allis 53214 (414) 844-1411 www.letmemakeyoublush.com

# 17. SEE THE SCULPTURE GARDEN ATOP THE GROHMANN MUSEUM

Open only during the warmer months, this is a must see for anyone who visits Milwaukee. The museum itself is quite extraordinary, but seeing Milwaukee from this roof top garden is heavenly. In total, 18 bronze sculptures of men and women toiling in the field and foundry, heaving hammers or pinching molten metal with hot tongs, are displayed in the Man at Work Collection. Each one is about 9 feet tall and weighs a thousand pounds. You will also find a beautiful mural and flowers in raised garden beds. Be sure to peek inside the dome at the stained glass windows.

Go to the basement first and hit up the vending machines. It's a rare occasion to get coffee for 50 cents and snacks for $1 or less. You can make your coffee break one of the most memorable. 1000 N. Broadway, Milwaukee 53202 (414) 277-2300 www.msoe.edu

# 18. TAKE A TOUR

It's always a good idea to learn more about the city where you live. A tour is a fun way to do this. Here are my favorites. Experts host some. Others are self-directed. Choose what fits your schedule and interests. Check Groupon and Living Social for discounts on these tours. Most also have Facebook pages where you can find additional information and last minute changes.

**Historic Milwaukee Inc.** Summer walking tours, led by passionate volunteers, take you into many of Milwaukee's neighborhoods. The tours are free if you become a member of HMI or $10 for non-members. Membership rates vary from $20 for a student to $35 for an individual. You can visit Historic Third Ward, Brady Street, North Point Mansions, or the Downtown. http://historicmilwaukee.org

**Milwaukee Food Tours.** Discover the sights and flavors of Milwaukee's most delicious neighborhoods. You'll eat as you hear stories on your tour of choice. Some are walking tours. Others take you by bus. They also offer a hop on/hop off bus, holiday tours to see Christmas lights, and a photo walk. www.milwaukeefoodtours.com

**Milwaukee Ghosts Tours & Investigations**. Tales of haunted history and folklore as you walk with a guide through the Third Ward, which used to be known as the "Bloody Third" when it was a ghetto where fistfights were commonplace. www.milwaukeeghosts.com

**Untapped Tours**. Touted as Milwaukee's most complete city tour, you ride an 11-passenger van through the city and learn more about the famous attractions, as well as some lesser-known places. The 3-hour Milwaukee tour takes you past mansions, landmarks, and includes stops at Clock

Shadow Creamery to sample cheese and Lakefront Brewery for a tour and beer tasting. Meet at City Hall. www.untappedtours.com

**Milwaukee Seven Seat Bike Tours.** Learn about Milwaukee's east side and hear ghastly, haunting topics, as you pedal with others on a "conference bike" along Lake Park and the surrounding neighborhood. Weekends departing from North and Prospect (next to Whole Foods). Online reservations. (414) 628-5103 www.sevenseatbike.com

**Hangman Tours.** These evening tours, based out of Shaker's Cigar Bar, take you walking through Milwaukee and are theme based: Shaker's Ghost, Cream City Cannibal (about Jeffrey Dahmer), The Milwauking Dead, and the Whoring 20's. Be sure to ask where your meet-up location will be. Tours come with a wristband that allows you a free drink at Shaker's afterwards. Be sure to take them up on it if you like history or haunted places. It's a beautiful bar that was once owned by Al Capone. They have theme dinners, magic acts, and live music. 422 S. 2nd St., Milwaukee 53204 www.hangmantours.com

**MMSD's Water Reclamation Facility.** Group tours for adults and older students at the Jones Island Water Reclamation Facility. Call (414) 747-3850. Central laboratory is also available to understand more about environmental testing in the state's largest municipal wastewater testing lab. Or maybe you want to ride the Pelagos Water Quality monitoring vessel. (414) 225- 2191 www.mmsd.com

**Milwaukee Soldiers' Home.** This is a self-guided tour of the Milwaukee Soldiers' Home National Historic Landmark district, which can be downloaded to your smart phone as an app. It's also helpful to print out the map, from the website, to use as a visual while you tour. Parking can be difficult to find on a weekday. The whole tour takes about 45 minutes. www.savethesoldiershome.com

**Milwaukee Architecture.** A retired professor of electrical engineering, Dr. Steven Reyer, put some amazing work into creating this self-guided tour. Download maps that take you through your selected part of the city (east or west). www.mequonsteve.com/mke/

**Historic Third Ward Walking Tour.** Download a self guided plan that takes you through the Historic Third Ward and includes details about many of the interesting buildings, often featured in movies. It's eight pages of fun history. http://www.historicthirdward.org/about/takeatour.php

**General Mitchell International Airport.** Do you love airplanes and airports? Our airport is full of interesting art, exhibits and even a museum. Download the self-guided tour and learn something new about aviation and our local airport. 5300 S. Howell Ave., Milwaukee 53207 (414) 747-5300 www.mitchellairport.com/files/5413/4003/6295/Self-Guided_Tour_Handout.pdf

# 19. SIP A LOCALLY-ROASTED COFFEE

Milwaukee is known for its beer, but recently it's receiving accolades for its perfectly roasted, fresh brewed coffee. We have four local roasters, so find a café and see which is your favorite spot.

**Anodyne Coffee**. A microroastery and retail café with locations in Bay View and Walker's Point. Plenty of outlets if you need to get some work done or just want to recharge your phone. 2920 S Kinnickinnic Ave., Milwaukee 53207 (414) 489-0765 224 W. Bruce St., Milwaukee 53204 (414) 763-1143 www.anodynecoffee.com

**Colectivo Coffee.** Not only do they have coffee, they have an amazing array of healthy salads, muffins, and wraps. They have 13 cafes, but my favorite locations are at the lakefront on a sunny day, or at the Bay View Café where you can watch the breads being made at their Troubadour bakery. 2301 S. Kinnickinnic Ave., Milwaukee 53207 (414) 744-6117. 1701 N. Lincoln Memorial Dr., Milwaukee 53202 (414) 223-4551 www.colectivocoffee.com

**Valentine Coffee Co.** The newest roaster in Milwaukee, they believe in quality small batch roasting. Rather than creating cafes all over Milwaukee, they have a coffee bar where you can watch them prepare your coffee. The barista will teach you more about coffee in three minutes than you ever thought possible. 5918 W. Vliet St., Milwaukee 53208 (414) 988-8018 www.valentinecoffeeco.com

**Stone Creek Coffee.** With ten cafes in the area, each manages to have its own personality. I like the Walker's Point café with its outdoor fire pits and music streaming from next door's Radio Milwaukee. 158 S. Barclay St., Milwaukee 53204 www.stonecreekcoffee.com

## 20. GO OUT FOR SUNDAY BRUNCH

Sunday mornings are made for brunch. The eggs taste better if you can eat outdoors during summer on a fine patio. Put in "Sunday brunch" on Yelp and you'll get about a hundred different spots. I'll just list some that consistently come up as favorites around town and haven't been mentioned other places in the book.

**Smyth at the Iron Horse Hotel.** One of the best brunches in town. Food is made with farm fresh ingredients that come from their own half-acre farm north of Milwaukee. Honey comes from the hotel's beehives. You'll find stations where you help yourself to a spectacular selection of items, but you can order off the Route 66 menu, which is included in the price. The dishes are inspired by locations along the iconic American trail. Be sure to check out the hotel lobby too. Great decor! 500 W. Florida St., Milwaukee 53204 (414) 374-4766 www.theironhorsehotel.com/smyth/

**Blue's Egg.** Often listed as the #1 spot, expect long waits. For an unusual meal, order the polenta and Yukon fries. For benedict lovers, know that the ham used is pulled which makes it just a bit more elegant. Portions are generous. 317 N. 76th St., Milwaukee 53213 (414) 299-3180 www.bluesegg.com

**Hubbard Park Lodge.** This rustic lodge is open for lumberjack family style brunch every Sunday. You can eat unlimited pancakes served up with bacon, fresh fruit, eggs, and good strong coffee or juice. The best part for most kids is the mini doughnuts. Tasty every time. The lodge overlooks the Milwaukee River in Hubbard Park. 3565 N. Morris Blvd., Shorewood 53211(414) 332-4207 www.hubbardlodge.com

**The National.** A good alternative to the crowded restaurants, this cozy café has brunch available every day. There is one dish you can only get on weekends and it's called the "Hot Mess"- a delicious egg concoction including potatoes, veggies, meat, and hollandaise. Go hungry! $10 goes a long way here. 839 W. National Ave., Milwaukee 53204 (414) 431-6551 www.nationaleats.com

**The Knick.** Some amazing eats here- crab cake benedict, breakfast pasta or polish sausage and eggs. The banana pecan pancakes with whisky butter- yumm! Eat out on the patio in nicer weather and enjoy a view of Lake Michigan. 1030 E. Juneau Ave., Milwaukee 53202 (414) 272-0011 www.theknickrestaurant.com

**Bartolotta's Lake Park Bistro.** Set in beautiful Lake Park, this is a great place to combine a meal with a stroll. They host a champagne brunch and have a kid friendly menu as well. 3133 E. Newberry Blvd., Milwaukee 53211 (414) 962-6300 www.lakeparkbistro.com

**Smoke Shack.** This tiny restaurant only has 47 seats, but they are famous for their meats. They also do an unusual hearty brunch. Biscuits and gravy, sweet potato pancakes, and pulled pork benedict with fried green tomatoes. 332 N. Milwaukee St., Milwaukee 53202 (414) 431-1119 www.smoke-shack.com

**Beans and Barley.** Smoothies, every egg option imaginable, and homemade bagels. Vegetarian and gluten free options. 1901 E. North Ave., Milwaukee 53202 (414) 278-7878 www.beansandbarley.com

**Café Hollander.** Great casual dining and very bike friendly. Some interesting combinations for pancakes and waffles keep us coming back. Be daring and try the chicken and cheddar jalapeno waffle! 2608 N. Downer Ave., Milwaukee 53211 (414) 963-6366 www.cafehollander.com

**Trocadero.** Try this French themed Gastrobar that serves mini donuts as a starter that melt in your mouth. You'll find interesting cheeses, veggies, and grains you won't find other places worked into egg dishes that delight. Come hungry! 1758 N. Water St., Milwaukee, 53202 (414) 272-0205 www.trocaderogastrobar.com

**Pizza Man.** I'll bet you never talked about pizza and brunch in the same sentence, but it can happen in Milwaukee! They do serve pizza, but also egg dishes cooked Italian style and a healthy vanilla-honey yogurt with granola. They also have one of the largest selections of wines and beers in the area. 2597 N. Downer Ave., Milwaukee 53211 (414) 272-1745 www.pizzamanmke.com

**Ma Fischer's.** Hearty portions of comfort food with incredibly fast service. You can get gyro meat with your breakfast. Open 24 hours with breakfast served all day to satisfy your late night hunger. 2214 N. Farwell Ave., Milwaukee 53202 (414) 271-7424 www.mafischersrestaurant.com

## 21. TOUR FOREST HOME CEMETERY

**Forest Home Cemetery** is the resting place for nearly everyone who contributed to making Milwaukee what it was in the early years of Milwaukee's history. It's listed on the National Register of Historic Places, and was declared a landmark in 1973. It's not just your average headstones you'll find in this garden cemetery either. Drive the winding roads that pass through English gardens and massive trees, and you'll see a wide variety of art forms. Spring brings flowers in abundance. Fall brings a palette of colors in the treetops since this is one of the most diverse arboretums in the state. There are decorative bridges and beautiful water features.

You can take a Sunday tour during the summer months with a guide who will focus on a theme relative to Milwaukee's history: Beer barons, women who made Milwaukee, mayors, and other notable Milwaukeeans. I guarantee you will learn something interesting. Call to find out about tours or to receive the newsletter.

If you can't make it to the tours given by docents, you can download a walking tour at their website. Be sure to stop in at the Halls of History (contact someone at the main office if it's locked) where you can see photos and stories of everyone buried here that had anything to do with early Milwaukee's story. Some of the people you may learn about: Arthur Oliver Smith, Frederick Pabst, Valentine Blatz, Joseph Schlitz, Frank Zeidler, and three of the Davidson family (Arthur, William, and Walter) of Harley Davidson fame. Even the Milwaukeean who invented the typewriter and the QWERTY keyboard, Christopher Sholes, is buried here. 2405 W. Forest Home Ave., Milwaukee 53215 (414) 645-2632 www.foresthomecemetery.com

## 22. SEE MORE THAN ANIMALS AT THE ZOO

**Milwaukee Zoo** is obviously a place to see animals in enclosures, but in recent years there is so much more. Maybe you've been there to ride the train, carousel, and sky safari, but there is a new SkyTrail ropes course and zip line, for an additional charge. To do the larger ropes course, you need to be 48" high. It requires a certain amount of courage.

Bring quarters so you can get a foot massage on the chairs found all over the grounds. You'll also need them at the petting zoo to buy goat food. The sea lion show is equal to anything you'll find at Sea World, but a lot cheaper and closer to home. You can eat a meal with the Easter bunny, attend a camp, eat your way through zoo a la carte, and listen to music outdoors all summer. Watch a performance of the Kohl's Wild Theater. Take a class in their education building with the growing green roof. Check their events page for the latest in fun. For adults who appreciate art, look for the sculptures, paintings, poetry displays, and topiary. More info at www.zoosociety.org, then click on "Planning Your Visit". There's a mobile app with a map called MILWAUKEE COUNTY ZOO downloadable at iTunes. With it you can see rides, attractions, and food. Discounts for Milwaukee county residents. 10001 W. Blue Mound Rd., Milwaukee 53226 (414) 771-3040 www.milwaukeezoo.org

## 23. GO INSIDE THE OLDEST CHAPEL IN THE USA

**St. Joan of Arc Chapel** has a long history, which began in the French countryside more than five centuries ago. It was in ruins when French architect Jacques Couelle, who meticulously documented it, found it in the 1920's. In 1926, Gertrude Hill Gavin, an American, acquired the chapel and brought it to her estate at Long Island. American architect John Russell Pope added the early Gothic altar and the famous Joan of Arc Stone when it was rebuilt. The story of the stone says that Joan of Arc (1412-1431) prayed before a statue of Our Lady standing on this stone and then kissed the stone. Ever since, that stone has been colder than surrounding stones.

It's a beautiful chapel with stained glass windows, placed at Marquette University in a raised garden since 1966. It is believed to be the only medieval structure in the entire Western Hemisphere dedicated to its original purpose. Take a free tour, offered every day of the week. You can also attend mass here. 1415 W. Wisconsin Ave., Milwaukee 53233 (414) 288-6873 www.marquette.edu/chapel/index.shtml

## 24. SEE THE CEILING AT BASILICA OF ST. JOSAPHAT

Milwaukee has plenty of beautiful churches filled with imported stained glass and beautiful paintings. One stands out among them as being the best of the best. **Basilica of St. Josaphat** is a religious building with an unconventional beginning. It was built using stones, which were salvaged from the Chicago Post Office and Custom House. $20,000 and 500 railroad flat cars were required to bring the materials to Milwaukee. Volunteers helped build this fantastic church, which rivals anything in Europe. It is in fact a smaller version of St. Peter's in Rome. The church has the same cross-shaped floor plan and huge central dome. Stained glass windows were imported from Austria. Murals were painted by Roman artist, Gonippo Raggi in 1926. It seats more than 1000 people on the main floor, while hundreds more can be seated in the galleries. The acoustics make listening to music here a real treat so attend Sunday Mass if you are able, and take the tour following Mass. Otherwise, stop by for a self-guided tour during visiting hours. You can download the visitor guide and tour at the website. 2333 S. 6th St., Milwaukee 53215 (414) 645-5623 www.thebasilica.org

## 25. TRY A WINTER SPORT

Milwaukee county parks are open for business even during the coldest winter days. Make the best of it by trying a winter activity that might be new to you. There are ice rinks, sledding hills, and ice fishing. Some equipment is available at the parks, so all you need is to bundle up and bring some enthusiasm. Check the events page all year long to find out what's happening. www.county.milwaukee.gov/parks

**Urban Ecology Center.** There are three branches with lending closets. For the biggest bang for your buck, become a member for less than $50 per year and you can borrow equipment all year round for free. This includes cross-country skis and boots, snowshoes, ice skates, sleds, and toboggans during winter. Washington Park (1859 N. 40th St.) has a skating rink, small hills for sledding, and lots of space to try out snowshoes and skis all in one day. Riverside Park (1500 E. Park Place) has hills and access to trails along the Milwaukee River. Menomonee Valley (3700 W. Pierce St.) has the entire Three Bridges Park and Hank Aaron Trail in its backyard. There is something for everyone. They also have a full winter calendar of activities so if you want to learn something new, you'll be in good hands. www.urbanecologycenter.org

**Whitnall Park** has a winter clubhouse concession where you can rent skis ($25 per day) and snowshoes ($20). They also sell snacks and drinks you can enjoy in front of the massive fireplace. If snow cover is inadequate, the clubhouse is closed. Bring your own sled and take a few runs down the sledding hill any time there is snowfall. 6751 S. 92nd St., Franklin, 53132

**Dog Sledding** is offered by the Door County Sled dogs during winter weekends at Whitnall Park, or at the lakefront across from Colectivo Coffee. These are rescued dogs that live with families and work together with volunteers. It's a fun ride around the park. Be sure to bring a camera. www.doorcountysleddogs.com

**Sledding.** The county maintains a number of sledding hills in the parks: Brown Deer, Columbus, Currie, Greene, Hales Corners, Humboldt, LaFollette, McCarty, McGovern, Pulaski, Wilson, and Whitnall. For park addresses go to www.county.milwaukee.gov/Sledding

**The Rock Sports Complex**. This is the area ski hill used for downhill skiing, snowboarding, and snow tubing. They make their own snow and provide a variety of terrain. Equipment and lessons are available. 7900 W. Crystal Ridge Dr., Franklin 53132 (414) 529-7676 www.rockcomplex.com

**Slice of Ice in Red Arrow Park.** Ice-skating on your lunch hour? Why not? Lockers and skate rental/sharpening are available. Starbucks coffee and bakery in the warming house await you. The refrigerated rink is lit and makes for a beautiful outdoor setting. There are additional rinks at county park lagoons. 920 N. Water St., Milwaukee 53202 (414) 289-8791 www.county.milwaukee.gov/redarrow11930.htm

**Pettit National Ice Center.** You don't have to wait for winter to strap on skates. With year round rinks available for curling, hockey and figure skating, you can join a team or just skate during a public skate session. This is a US Olympic training site so you may spot some local Olympians practicing. While you're there, check out the National Speedskating Museum and Hall of Fame for a little inspiration. 500 S. 84th St., Milwaukee 53214 www.thepettit.com

**Milwaukee Curling Club.** The Milwaukee Curling Club is actually based in nearby Cedarburg. This is the longest running curling club in the US. They can introduce you to the sport and put you on a team if you enjoy it. Ozaukee County Fairgrounds, W67 N890 Washington Ave., Cedarburg 53012 www.milwaukeecurlingclub.com

**Ice Fishing** is allowed in several county park lagoons when the ice is at least 6 inches thick. There are usually free fishing clinics offered for children at some point during the winter. For more information about the lagoons that are stocked and used for ice fishing, check the county parks website. www.county.milwaukee.gov/icefishing10254.htm

# 26. WATCH A SUNRISE AT LAKE MICHIGAN

Get down to the lakefront early and watch the sunrise as it comes up over Lake Michigan. You never know what you're going to see. Sometimes there are gorgeous hues of red and yellow. Other times, you might not see anything but fog and clouds. Don't let the cold stop you! Bradford Beach and the other northerly beaches are beautiful once the ice freezes into formations, and you can show up a bit later than in summer.

## 27. FIND A GREEN ROOF

In the past few years, there are more green roofs topping public buildings because they make so much sense for a city trying to reduce storm water runoff. A green roof can capture and hold hundreds or even thousands of gallons of water, add insulation to the building, and cut heating and cooling bills. Learn more about green roofs at www.freshcoast740.com. There are many more green roofs than those I've listed, but most aren't accessible or can't be seen.

The one above in the photo can be seen at 35th and National if you step onto the 35th street Bridge. The sheep add a certain charm to it. If you're there, go underneath the bridge and see the sheep inspired mural painted and designed by Reynaldo Hernandez and a group of students working with ArtWorks for Milwaukee.

**Milwaukee Central Library**. Take a guided tour of the 33,000 square foot green roof above the Business and Periodicals Room. You can touch a sample of the roof materials, see the sedum growing, and learn about the energy saving solar panels. Meet in the library's main lobby Wednesdays at noon and Saturdays at 10 am, April through October. 814 W. Wisconsin Ave., Milwaukee 53233 (414) 286-2797 www.mpl.org/about/green_roof/

**Clock Tower Shadow Building.** CORE/El Centro clients, staff, and volunteers maintain the gardens and green roof at the top of this building. Come for workshops or a farmer's market and enjoy the view. You can even rent the rooftop for your special event. 138 W. Bruce St., Milwaukee 53204 (414) 225-4267 www.core-elcentro.org/garden-nutrition

**Riverside Park Urban Ecology Center.** This was one of the first green projects in Milwaukee. The entire building is made with recycled materials and solar powered. The toilets made some pretty interesting lists because of the unique rainwater flush system. "14 places you have to poop at before you die" comes to mind. Access the flowering green roof from the second floor and be sure to climb the tower for a great view. 1500 E. Park Pl., Milwaukee 53211 (414) 964-8505

**Menomonee Valley Urban Ecology Center.** This small roof has a couple of chairs, some pretty flowers, and a bee box. 3700 W. Pierce St., Milwaukee 532215 (414) 431-2940 www.urbanecologycenter.org

**Rockwell Automation Building.** Probably the only time you'd notice the roof on top of this building, which earned a green building certification, is when you get up into the Allen Bradley clock tower. Doors Open Milwaukee holds an annual event, which might include this tour (www.doorsopenmilwaukee.org). The roof is covered in 12 varieties of sedum, spiderwort, native onion, native chives, and black-eyed susans. 1201 S. 2nd St., Milwaukee 53204 (414) 382-2000 www.rockwellautomation.com

**MSOE Athletic Field and Parking Complex.** This three level parking structure has a field on top for collegiate soccer, lacrosse, rugby and youth sports. It has the first all LED lit competition field in the US, which saves energy and is dimmable. This roof reduces the heat island effect that comes from asphalt. 1305 N. Broadway, Milwaukee 53202

**Braise Restaurant.** This unique farm to table restaurant has a rooftop garden where they grow greens and herbs during the summer months. The menu indicates what was plucked from the rooftop. The menu changes frequently depending on what is available, which makes it fun to visit often. You can take a seat with a view of the Allen Bradley clock, but make a reservation to be sure you get priority seating. Food is fresh, creative, and delicious! 1101 S. 2nd St., Milwaukee 53204 (414) 212-8843 www.braiselocalfood.com

**Tochi.** At this Asian fusion restaurant, there is a rooftop lounge where you can see what's blooming while you enjoy a drink. 2107 E. Capitol Dr., Shorewood, 53211 (414) 963-9510. www.tochimke.com

**Radio Milwaukee 88Nine.** Every Thursday at 4:30 you can take a behind the scenes tour, which includes the 2500 square foot roof. The building is also interesting- a manufacturing building featuring barn wood from a Sheboygan dairy. Click on radio Milwaukee tours on their website under events to sign up. 220 E. Pittsburg Ave., Milwaukee 53203 www.radiomilwaukee.org

## 28. GET MORE THAN GOOD BOOKS
## AT CENTRAL LIBRARY

We can certainly be proud of our local library-one of the most beautiful libraries in the nation. The building itself was designed in a competition where Frank Lloyd Wright was one of the losers! You can imagine the keen competition. When designed by Ferry & Clas, it was meant to house both the museum and library. It stayed that way from 1898 through the mid 1960s when the museum was moved to Wells Street. Everything above ground is pretty impressive, but you don't see four levels below ground that house books.

It has a café where you can get a sandwich and a coffee while you browse the used books for sale. Children can climb a lighthouse or put on their own puppet shows. There is even a drive-up window. Tour this historic building any Saturday with a member of the Library Friends group. Meet in the rotunda at 1:30. 814 W. Wisconsin Ave., Milwaukee 53233 (414) 286-3000. www.mpl.org

## 29. VISIT AN ART GALLERY

Milwaukee has become quite the artists' city in recent years. Our Historic Third Ward is often compared to New York's SoHo neighborhood. Featuring six square blocks filled with art galleries, theaters, boutiques, and specialty stores, it has become the hub of artistic activity.

With more than 100 art spaces listed on Yelp, you can certainly find an eclectic mix. These are not pretentious places where you feel unwelcome. Attend a Gallery Night or browse a few to see what I mean. Most have items for sale, but others just display local artists' fare. The universities in our area have art programs, so naturally you'll find some talented students featuring their artwork. Admission is free to most galleries. Here are just a few to get you started.

**Art & Soul Gallery.** A contemporary gallery with colorful paintings on every wall and interesting furniture topped with pottery, glassworks, and jewelry. This is a gallery, but so much more. Affordable art for any budget. They also have a space you can rent for private functions. 5708 W. Vliet St., Milwaukee 53208 (414) 774-4185 www.artsoul-gallery.com

**Marshall Building.** With seven floors of artist studios, galleries, and workshops, this is a very creative space. The 3$^{rd}$ Friday of the month is an open house where you can meet the artists and see their work. 207 E. Buffalo St., Milwaukee 53202 www.marshallbuildingmke.com

**David Barnett Gallery.** An eclectic gallery in the beautiful Button Mansion featuring the art of more than 600 artists from far and near. It has a national reputation for its extensive collection of Picasso ceramics and Milton Avery oil paintings. Attending an exhibition here is a real treat for art lovers. You'll believe you're in a large city like New York. 1024 State St., Milwaukee 53202 (414) 271-5058 www.davidbarnettgallery.com

**The Pitch Project.** A contemporary art gallery that also houses artist studios. They feature art and programs. What makes this kind of extraordinary? One of the co-founders, Mike Brenner, started a brewery to support the arts in a roundabout way. He decided since people came and saw art while having a few drinks, they might as well be drinking his beer. You have to experience this grassroots effort first hand to truly appreciate it. 706 S. 5th St., Milwaukee www.thepitchproject.org

**Walker's Point Center for the Arts.** Set in a historic 1885 building made of cream city brick, you'll find local artists and art featured in this neighborhood gallery. The center serves more than 10,000 kids every year. If you're a local artist, you can enter the juried art show. 839 S. Fifth St., Milwaukee 53204 (414) 672-2787 www.wpca-milwaukee.org

**Milwaukee Institute of Art & Design.** The Jane Bradley Pettit building, which is MIAD's main campus, has two nationally recognized museum galleries: the Brooks Stevens Gallery of Industrial Design and the Frederick Layton Gallery. They often host professional and student displays. 273 E. Erie St., Milwaukee 53202 (414) 847-3200. www.miad.edu

**UWM Art Galleries.** There are four galleries associated with Peck School of the Arts. Admission is always free. www.uwm.edu/psoa/

INOVA- Institute of Visual Arts is a space where artistic research and collaboration take place. (2155 N. Prospect)

Arts Center Gallery serves as a teaching and professional research laboratory. Exhibits rotate monthly during the school year. (2400 E. Kenwood Blvd Arts building, 2nd floor)

UWM Student Union shows a variety of works with changing exhibits throughout the school year. Check their exhibits page to see what's on now. (2200 E. Kenwood Blvd, UWM Student Union Room W199)

UWM Art History Gallery houses the UWM permanent art collection of 7000 artworks, which include a diverse selection of paintings, prints, sculptures, and decorative arts. You'll find some big names here: O'Keefe, Renoir, Warhol, and Picasso to name a few. It's being renovated in 2014 so that it will have a space doubled in size when it reopens in 2015. (3203 N. Downer Ave., Mitchell Hall, Room 154)

**Art Bar.** If you like good music and local art on display, this lively place in Riverwest might be for you. Lots of games. It's a dog friendly bar too. 722 E. Burleigh St., Milwaukee 53212 (414) 372-7880

# 30. MAKE YOUR OWN ART

Why not make something with your own two hands? Paint, mold, draw, or blow to make something unique. Check with your local Parks & Recreation guide, or try one of these fun places.

**Artist and Display.** This is the kind of place you walk through and want one of everything. They have supplies you might need to make…well, anything! They also have classes in a variety of arts, both for kids and adults. Learn how to paint, draw, cartoon or even zentangle. Locally owned and operated family business since 1936. 9015 W. Burleigh St., Milwaukee 53222 (414) 442-9100 www.artistanddisplay.com

**Splash Studio.** A painting bar with three hour guided sessions, hosted by an artist, ensures you have a masterpiece to take home with you. Check the website to book a date based on the painting you want to try. Though everyone is making the same picture, they are all unique. 184 N. Broadway, Milwaukee 53202 (414) 882-7621 www.splashmilwaukee.com

**Milwaukee Blacksmith, Inc**. Learn to work with iron under the supervision of a seasoned blacksmith, and go home with your finished project. 518 E. Erie, Milwaukee 53202 (414) 241-4911

**Murray Hill Pottery Works.** Sit at the wheel and play while teachers help you make your very own bowl. 2456 N. Murray Ave., Milwaukee 53211 (414) 332-8828 www.murrayhillpottery.com

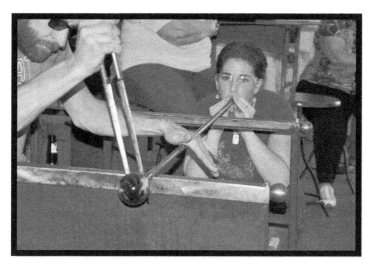

**Square One Art Glass.** Learn how to blow glass (above). All materials are provided. This makes for a fun outing with a group of friends. The studio gets quite warm so dress in layers. 5322 W. Vliet St., Milwaukee 53208 (414) 259-0811 www.squareoneartglass.com

**Art Trooper.** At this make-it-yourself art studio, you can do glass fusing, paint pottery, and create mosaics. 333 W. Brown Deer Rd., Fox Point, 53217 (414) 351-1855 www.arttrooper.com

**Daly's Pen Shop**. Maybe you like writing or calligraphy. Just step inside America's oldest pen shop! You will find everything you need…and probably more! 7632 W. Burleigh St., Milwaukee 53222 (866) 574-9572

**Milwaukee Makerspace.** An innovative workshop where people can pursue their creative interests. You can visit them on a Tuesday or Thursday at 7 PM during their public access times. It's free and will surely be inspiring. Their members have interests in diverse topics including electronics, robots, welding, music, art, video, textiles…and the list goes on. Feel free to bring a project you're working on for some advice. If you become a member, you'll have access to tools you probably don't have at home. They also offer classes in some useful and unusual hobbies and crafts. Access the courses at their website. 2555 S. Lenox St., Milwaukee 53207 www.milwaukeemakerspace.org

**Lynden Sculpture Garden.** This is a park-like setting with indoor and outdoor exhibits. You can find a wide variety of workshops for all ages. Check the upcoming events. 2145 W. Brown Deer Rd., Milwaukee 53217 (414) 446-8794 www.lyndensculpturegarden.org

**AWE, Inc.** Go to a local park or library with your kids to make some art, or hire their mobile art studio for your next event. 4315 W. Vliet St., Milwaukee 53208 (414) 933-3877 www.awe-inc.org

## 31. TOUR GROWING POWER AND TRY SOME MICROGREENS

Will Allen has become somewhat of a global phenomenon since starting **Growing Power**, the urban garden in Milwaukee. It's not only a place to grow food and raise livestock; it's a place he believes transforms the community. People from diverse backgrounds living nearby can enjoy healthy, affordable food.

Learn about the variety of foods grown and how the foods are distributed to local restaurants, as well as the Growing Power Café. You can see mushrooms growing out of feedbags hung from the ceiling. Find dozens of trays of nutrient packed microgreens, which are the baby version of spinach, lettuce, kale and other vegetables. They create tons of compost and soil with the help of waste and worms. In a three-tiered system, they grow tilapia and silver lake perch in large tanks buried four feet in the ground. Water from the tanks, filled with the nutrients from the fishes' waste, is pulled up to feed the plants above it- tomatoes on the top level and watercress on the middle level. The fish fertilize the plants, and the plants filter the water.

Public tours are offered Monday through Sunday at 1:00, and last 1-½ hours. Cost is $10. Maybe this will inspire you to start growing your own veggies. 5500 W. Silver Spring Dr., Milwaukee 53218 (414) 527-1546 www.growingpower.org

**Central Greens** is another interesting place where microgreens and herbs are being grown using fish waste in a system called aquaponics. Take a tour or support them by picking up these greens for your next salad or smoothie at Outpost or other local grocery stores. 470 N. Storyhill Pl., Milwaukee 53208 (414) 302-9495 www.milwaukeeaquaponics.com

## 32. DO THE DOMES AT MITCHELL PARK

You can see the three huge domes in Mitchell Park from most places in the valley. The official name is the Mitchell Park Conservatory, and it has been part of the Milwaukee scene since 1898. Back then the original conservatory housed flowers in a greenhouse setting. The domes you see now were built in phases between 1959 and 1967. It's the only complex like this in the world! These let you experience a desert oasis, tropical jungle, and special exhibits with flowers. There's also a brand new greenhouse area so that the flowers displayed can be grown right on site. During winter you'll find concerts, beach parties, and a farmer's market. During summer, come for the special exhibits and the art festival. Every Monday morning is free admission for Milwaukee county residents. The gift shop has something for anyone interested in nature, horticulture, or Wisconsin in general. It's a small space with some great finds, so be sure to check it out. 524 S. Layton Blvd., Milwaukee 53215 (414) 257-5611 www.milwaukeedomes.org

# 33. PLAY GOLF INDOORS OR OUT

Why is someone kicking a soccer ball in the above photo? It's because there are more ways to play golf in Milwaukee than just the traditional sport. All these golf options are available at several Milwaukee County Parks. Book a tee time and find out about specials at this website www.milwaukeecountygolfcourses.com

**Traditional golf.** There are 15 courses to choose from. You can also join a league or play with a group.

**Foot Golf.** Bring your own soccer ball or rent one at the course. A great family sport, you kick the ball to large holes, marked by flags, on a golf course shared with traditional golfers. The kids love riding in the cart.

**Nite-Glow Golf.** Played after dark, the ball glows so you can find it. For even more fun, stop at **American Science & Surplus** (6901 W. Oklahoma, Milwaukee 53219) to find everything you need in neon light sticks, jewelry, etc. and get decked out for play.

**Disc Golf.** Using a plastic disc, you throw it into metal baskets made of chains. http://county.milwaukee.gov/DiscFrisbeeGolf9008.htm

**Indoor Golf.** Currie Park has a heated indoor driving range with 33 hitting bays for practice or lessons. 3535 N. Mayfair Rd., Wauwatosa (414) 453-1742 www.curriegolfdome.com

**FORE! Milwaukee**. An indoor golf experience in the heart of downtown that offers lessons, hitting bays and four hitting simulators. 530 N. Water St., Milwaukee 53202 (414) 272-FORE www.foremilwaukee.com

# 34. LISTEN TO ORGAN OR PIANO MUSIC

**Lucille's Piano Bar & Grill.** Two pianos are front and center. The pianists play requests, and make up songs for special guests that are very entertaining. Bring cash if you want to make a request. This is a popular place for bachelorette parties. They have specialty drinks like a Jell-O shot with whipped cream, or a fish bowl with multiple straws. This is the place to get the party started. You can sing along. 1110 N. Old World Third St., Milwaukee 53203 (414) 225-0304 www.lucillesmke.com

**Angelo's Lounge.** This is a much quieter venue with a corner piano. It's intimate enough that you're likely to know everyone in the place before you leave. You'll find the regulars take the microphone, celebrities drop in to play guitar or piano, and the talented bartender croons any song that is played. The walls are adorned in autographed photos by the likes of Tom Jones. If you have a break in the music, you can play the jukebox and get 4 songs for $1! Cash only. 1686 N. Van Buren St., Milwaukee 53244 www.angelospianolounge.com

**Oriental Theatre.** This historic movie theatre still has an organist play the Kimball Theatre Pipe Organ every Friday and Saturday before the 7 PM show in the main theatre. You can enjoy cocktails, fancy coffee, and tasty popcorn during the movie. This place is a real treat, decorated with lions and East Indian decor. 2230 N. Farwell Ave., Milwaukee 53202 (414) 276-5140 www.landmarktheatres.com/Market/Milwaukee/OrientalTheatre.htm

**Organ Piper Pizza.** This unique family pizza place plays organ music on an early 1900s Wurlitzer theater pipe organ every day except Monday, when they are closed. As the organ plays, ducks join in the chorus, and other musical antics go off around the room. There's a Dixie band every first Wednesday night. Kids love the game room and mini carousel. 4353 S. 108th St., Greenfield 53228 (414) 529-1177 www.organpiperpizza.com

## 35. SEE A FILM AT A FILM FESTIVAL

Milwaukee is loaded with film talent. The rest of the world is just starting to appreciate that, but Milwaukeeans enthusiastically support the arts. One way is by putting warm bodies in seats to watch great films. We still get the traditional first run films at the chain theaters, but what makes us special are the great variety of original films made by locals, indie films, and foreign films offered during a festival.

Often you can find "after parties" at some fine Milwaukee hotels and restaurants. Browse this selection of festivals and see what might interest you. There are also language specific film festivals, such as French and Italian. Now it's your turn to put your hot body in a seat for one of our great film festivals!

**Milwaukee Underground.** A student-run international film festival showcasing contemporary works of film and video that innovate in form, technique, and content. Mitchell Hall B70, 3203 N. Downer Ave., Milwaukee 53211 (414) 229-6015 www.film-milwaukee.org

**Jewish Film.** A multi-day fall festival featuring films made by Jewish filmmakers, or about topics of interest to the Jewish community. Shows are played at Marcus North Shore Cinema, but tickets must be prepurchased through the Jewish Community Center, or at a table set up 30 minutes before show time. 11700 N. Port Washington Rd., Mequon. www.jccmilwaukee.org/filmfestival

**Milwaukee LGBT Film/Video.** Put on annually by the Peck School of the Arts, department of film. This used to span 4 days in October, but has grown to 11 days. Opening night at the Oriental Theatre. Others play at Union Theatre in UWM Union, 2200 E. Kenwood Blvd., Milwaukee 53211. www.arts.uwm.edu/lgbtfilm

**Milwaukee Film.** Held every fall with movies shown in four historic theaters, you will definitely find something to watch. Seeing the movies in these interesting spaces only adds to the experience. Buy individual tickets, a festival pass, volunteer, or become a member to get even more benefits. These shows often sell out, so browse the festival guide in advance and make your purchases early to ensure you get to see what you want. www.mkefilm.org

**Milwaukee Short Film.** The longest running Milwaukee film festival that supports Milwaukee filmmakers. Held in early September at Lubar Auditorium at the Milwaukee Art Museum, this festival spotlights emerging artists and focuses on the talent of Midwest filmmakers. 700 Art Museum Dr., Milwaukee 53202 http://festival.milwaukeeindependentfilmsociety.org

**48-Hour Film Project Milwaukee.** This is an international competition that runs in many cities where anyone can make a movie alone or with a team. Filmmakers pull a genre from a hat and are assigned three required elements for their film; a prop, a line of dialogue, and a character. They have only 48 hours to complete the film, which is then judged by a panel of experts. At the end of the project, movies are selected for a special screening night and awards are given. The best film moves on to compete at Filmapalooza in Los Angeles, and hopefully on to the Cannes Film Festival. www.48hourfilm.com/milwaukee

## 36. GRILL A SAUSAGE

Brats are a tradition in Milwaukee, but what kind? A variety of ethnic traditions fill our meat markets, so this could potentially mean any type of sausage. Everyone has his or her own secret recipe. Some like them soaked before grilling. Others think it's all about the toppings. Load it up with jalapenos, sauerkraut, cheese, and mustard. Put it in a pretzel bun or wrap it in bacon. The possibilities seem endless. Take them with you for picnics at the park or a tailgate party. Here's where Milwaukee shops for the widest fresh choices.

**Usinger's.** German style sausage and smoked meats, made in Milwaukee since 1880. They experiment with all kinds of brats. You'll even find recipes on their website. 1030 N. Old World 3$^{rd}$ St., Milwaukee 53203. (414) 276-9100 www.usinger.com

**Bunzel's Old Fashioned Meat Market.** High quality meats at good prices. You can buy in bulk here too. They also sell other groceries for one stop shopping. 8415 W. Burleigh St., Milwaukee 53222 www.bunzels.com

**European Homemade Sausage Shop.** You'll smell hickory as you walk in the door. This shop's specialty is Polish style sausages. You can even order online and have them shipped. Open Thursday-Saturday. 1985 South Muskego Ave., Milwaukee 53204 (414) 384-7320 www.eurosausage.com

**Sendiks.** Started by the Balistreri family 75 years ago, it has grown to 12 local markets. You can find turkey, pork, beef, and even chicken sausages made fresh daily with natural seasonings. www.sendiks.com

## 37. EAT LOCALLY MADE CHEESE

**Clock Shadow Creamery** is the only urban cheese factory in Milwaukee, and they have already won awards for their products. Stop by their store and pick up delicious cheeses made with milk from goats, sheep, and cows. If you're lucky, you'll get to see the cheese being made through the large window behind the cashier.

Take a cheese making tour where you can learn about the history of cheese and sample some fresh cheeses. Tours are $3 for adults and $1.50 for children. The tour is limited to the observation room, so it's more of a talk than a tour. Tours take about half an hour and are offered every half hour, but you need a reservation.

The building also has an interesting history. Considered one of the greenest buildings in the region, it was once an abandoned, contaminated lot before Juli Kaufmann decided to have it built with mostly salvaged materials. The building includes a geothermal heating and cooling system, rooftop garden, rainwater reuse system, a power generating building, and much more. The tenants all add to the community's services and include a free clinic, natural healing center, and law offices, which pride themselves on fighting for social and economic justice in Milwaukee. This is a building we can all be proud to have in our city. 138 W. Bruce St., Milwaukee 53204 (414) 273-9711 www.clockshadowcreamery.com

## 38. GET ON THE BUS

Taking the Milwaukee County Transit system is an experience you need to have. It's freeing to know you have options. Car not cooperating? Garage door frozen shut? You can still get to work. Want to bring your bike downtown? Put it on the rack at the front of the bus. You like festivals but hate paying $20 for parking? Take the bus. You can do it and they make it so easy. Routes and schedules are available on-line, as well as a color-coded system map. There's even a trip planner where you enter your starting and ending location.

You can also use your smart phone in Google maps. Just select the bus option and it will list the next bus number and tell you how long it will take. Sometimes it even gives you options, and tells you where to change buses, if necessary.

Once you're on the bus, there's an information center visible to passengers that tells you the next intersection. When you're ready to get off, just pull the cord. Easy peasy! Some seats are reserved for strollers or wheelchairs so be kind and allow access to these spaces.

Buy a bus pass at many locations around town or pay exact change with the driver. www.ridemcts.com

## 39. FIND THE CITY'S LARGEST COLLECTION OF AUTOGRAPHS

The Newsroom Pub and Milwaukee Press Club are co-located at the Safe House. This is the oldest continuing press club in North America, and maybe even the world! That's kind of a big deal. What's even bigger is that nearly every president has been here, along with many other dignitaries, and left their signatures. More than 1200 signatures date back to the 1890s. Who do you recognize? 137 E. Wells St., Milwaukee 53202. (414) 273-4900

## 40. RIDE A CHILI PEPPER OR A BULL

La Perla has a red chili pepper ride in their front window, and another in the tequila bar. They will handle an adult, but are tame enough for kids. Put on a sombrero, deposit a quarter in the coin box, and push the button. You're off on a Chili Pepper ride! A family friendly restaurant in the heart of Milwaukee's Latin Quarter. Be sure to try a margarita on the upstairs patio in nicer weather. 734 S. 5th St., (414) 645-9888 www.laperlahot.com

For the older, more adventurous crowd, go to Red Rock Saloon and see how many seconds you can ride the mechanical bull. Bring $5 and they will set you up! Good BBQ and rock/country dance music here. 1227 N. Water St., (414) 431-0467 www.redrockmilwaukee.com

## 41. TRY YOUR LUCK AT THE CASINO

Very few people get rich at a casino, but you can have fun trying. With 100 table games, a bingo hall, nearly 3000 slot machines, poker, off-track betting, entertainment and seven restaurants, there must certainly be something for everyone. A newly constructed 19-story hotel with 381 rooms only adds to the mix.

If you've never been to a casino, a fun place to start might be the Bingo Hall. You can either use paper or an electronic device that tracks the numbers called, making it a breeze to manage multiple cards. For about $20 you can play Breakfast Bingo for a couple of hours and drink free coffee.

There are lessons in how to play various games on the casino website, so don't go without reviewing the rules if you're new to the games. There are special events ongoing so check the schedule there. 1721 West Canal Street, Milwaukee 53233 (800) PAYSBIG www.paysbig.com

# 42. EAT SOME MILWAUKEE CHOCOLATE

We love our chocolate and we know how to create a unique experience! From truffles to drinking chocolate, there's something for everyone. Some of these are shops and others are chocolatiers who make their products but sell them to local businesses for retail. You will want to find these for gift giving.

**Red Elephant.** The smell inside this Historic Third Ward café is fabulous. You can choose desserts to eat with coffee, or just have a hot chocolate drink. There are truffles, hand painted chocolates, and all sorts of nuts and fruits dipped in chocolate. 333 N. Broadway St., Milwaukee 53202 (855) 733-3574 www.redelephant.com

**Northern Chocolate Co.** People describe the dark chocolate mint meltaways as best in the world, and I'd have to agree. Everything is nicely wrapped in cello bags. It's only open Friday-Saturday, so check the hours before you go. You'll have to ring the bell to enter. 2034 N Martin Luther King Jr. Dr., Milwaukee 53212 (414) 372-1885

**Burke Candy.** Not just chocolate is made here. You can also find amazing toffee in so many varieties. The turtles are another tasty treat. Family owned and operated using some of the secret family recipes like the salted caramels. This will not disappoint. 3840 N. Fratney St., Milwaukee 53212 (414) 964-7327 www.burkecandy.com

**Kehr's Candies.** Since 1930, they have been making hand dipped chocolates. There is a seasonal factory store, but you can purchase every day at the Milwaukee Public Market. 400 N. Water St., Milwaukee 53202 (414) 223-4305 www.kehrs.com

**Indulgence Chocolatiers.** Who would have thought you could pair chocolate and cheese? Chocolate and whiskey? Chocolate and beer? This creative place will take your taste buds on a tour. There are actually two locations, but I recommend you start with the pairing bar in Walker's Point neighborhood, where they often use local brewers, distilleries, and Clock Shadow Creamery to showcase Milwaukee's great products. The second location is in Shorewood. You can also pick up gift boxes wrapped in pretty ribbon containing a variety of truffles. Julie Waterman, owner/chocolatier, and her team make everything by hand in her shop, using only the finest chocolate. 211 S. 2nd St., Milwaukee 53204 (414) 223-0123 www.indulgencechocolatiers.com

**Chocobella.** With creations like shoes and hats, this is a unique place to get your chocolate fix. They also have some unusual flavors you won't find in the grocery store- habanero spiced peanut butter cups and guava. Yumm. Everything is a delight to the eyes and taste buds. Great for gift giving. 2474 S. Kinnickinnic Ave., Milwaukee 53207 (414) 747-9007 www.chocobella.net

**Tabal Chocolate.** This is the only organic chocolate producer in the state of Wisconsin, with the goal of making the best chocolate you have ever tasted. It's worth your time to seek out a bar and try it. Buy the bars at locations throughout the city, such as Outpost Natural Foods, Amaranth Bakery, or Beans & Barley. 3329 W. Lisbon Ave., Milwaukee 53208 www.tabalchocolate.com

**Omanhene.** Extraordinary gourmet chocolate and hot cocoa from Ghana, but the headquarters is in Milwaukee. Why Ghana? I checked with founder Steve Wallace. As a young man he was an exchange student in Ghana and came back to start this company as an adult, remembering what he had seen and wanting to make a difference. You can buy some at Anodyne Coffee Roasting Co. or other places around the city. 2290 S. Kinnickinnic Ave., Milwaukee 53207 (414) 276-8081 www.omanhene.com

## 43. SEE MILWAUKEE FROM THE LAKE

Often called the Third Coast, cities surrounding Lake Michigan seem to have more in common with coastal cities that sit on the oceans. We have beaches and a great view from the water of our fair Milwaukee. Here are a few options, just in case you don't have your own private yacht and captain. These are always more fun when shared with a few friends. The first three companies listed leave from the river, so you have the added benefit of seeing our beautiful bridges as they open for you.

**Milwaukee Boat Line.** Offering sightseeing with cocktails and music, this tour originates on the river and takes you out to the lake on a double decker boat. 101 W. Michigan St., Milwaukee 53203 (414) 294-9450 www.mkeboat.com

**Milwaukee River Cruise Line.** Take a public cruise with the largest fleet variety in Milwaukee. There are many themes to choose from - everything from history to a kids' pirate cruise complete with water fights. Many offer dinner options. They also rent pontoon boats. 205 W. Highland Blvd. Suite 204 Milwaukee 53203 (414) 276-7447 www.edelweissboats.com

**Riverwalk Boat Tours & Rentals.** Go out for a brewery tour or watch the sun set over the city. There are different themes daily. Pontoon rentals too. Pere Marquette Park, 950 Old World Third St., Milwaukee 53202 (414) 283-9999 www.riverwalkboats.com

**Sea Dog Sailing, LLC.** Excursions depart from Milwaukee's McKinley Marina from May-October. Try 90-minute public day sails or a 2-hour sunset cruise on a 38-foot yacht. You can either sit back and relax, or help sail. (414) 687-3203 www.seadogsailingmilwaukee.com

**Denis Sullivan.** This recreation of a 19th century schooner is a floating environmental classroom. Educational tours are 2-3 hours. Dress casually so you can help with the sails. 500 N. Harbor Dr., Milwaukee 53202 (414) 765-9966 www.discoveryworld.org

# 44. TOUR A MANSION

Milwaukee still has some beautiful mansions left over from the era of industrialists and beer barons. Just drive along Terrace Avenue from Lake Drive to see a wide variety of restored homes built in the 1800s and early 1900s. Each is unique.

To understand the lifestyles of the rich and famous of yesteryear, you need to peek inside. What most people notice first is the amazing amount of wood used inside for paneling, fireplaces, and decoration. Some of these historic homes have been turned into museums, like the Villa Terrace and Charles Allis Art Museums. Others are open to the public and are maintained like homes from that era.

**Pabst Mansion.** This is the home to Milwaukee's pioneer brewing family, which was restored to original condition. Open daily for tours, and for special events. Go at Christmas for the Dickens dinner (above) if you are able. You'll be delighted at all the decoration throughout the house. 2000 W. Wisconsin Ave., Milwaukee 53233 (414) 931-0808 www.pabstmansion.com

**Schuster Mansion.** Formerly the home of tobacco industrialist, George J. Schuster, now operating as a bed & breakfast, you can still tour the mansion and have high tea there. 3209 W. Wells St., Milwaukee (414) 342-3210 www.schustermansion.com

**Brumder Mansion.** A former home to newspaper publisher, George Brumder, now it's a bed & breakfast billed as Milwaukee's most romantic inn. Get a room or see a murder mystery show here. 3046 W. Wisconsin Ave., Milwaukee 53208 (414) 342-9767 www.milwaukeebedbreakfast.com

## 45. BE THE LIVE AUDIENCE FOR
## A RADIO SHOW

Want to feel a brush with fame?  Our local radio station, 88 NINE-Radio Milwaukee, has a program every Thursday at 5:30 PM called 414 Music.  Local artists and bands are invited to play in front of a studio audience, and the program is on live.  You don't need to reserve a seat.  Just show up and be ready to listen to some good music.  As part of the program, you're likely to learn a bit more about the artists, hear a couple of their popular songs, and maybe meet their families.  Often they have CDs or other merchandise for sale.

Since this building also houses Stone Creek Coffee, feel free to grab a drink and bring it into the studio. 220 E. Pittsburgh Ave., Milwaukee 53204 (414) 892-8899 www.radiomilwaukee.org

## 46. SHOP THE ETHNIC GROCERS

Milwaukee is diverse, but has been noted as one of the most segregated cities. When you only hang out in your own neighborhood, you miss out on some good culture!

Get outside your normal shopping area, and seek out one of our ethnic grocery stores. You'll be dazzled by colors, smells, and sounds you don't experience in a large chain. Meet the people who run them - all are family owned and operated. The best part? Lots of unusual choices and you could save a bundle, especially on produce.

**Pete's Fruit Market.** Walk in and hear the light, fun music. See the many flags representing Pete's customers. The smell of ripe produce fills your nostrils. It's a partying place serving the community, which is largely Hispanic. Service is fantastic. Try a fresh squeezed juice made to order. Assistance with groceries to your car is available. They even have on-line fruit baskets. 1400 S. Unions St., Milwaukee 53204 (414) 383-1300. www.petesfruitmarket.com

**Asian International Market.** This is the place to find authentic products from Southeast Asia, as well as the freshest papaya salad you're ever going to taste. The sisters who run this can help you with recipe ideas and suggest a unique sauce for your dishes. Walk the aisles and take in the sights before making your purchase. The deli serves up a variety of tasty dishes. 3401 W. National Ave., Milwaukee 53211 (414) 383-4188 www.asianinternationalmarket.com

**El Rey Family Market.**   The local neighborhood Hispanic grocery stores are in four locations.  They serve up a variety of Mexican dishes in the café at El Rey Family Market at very reasonable prices. You get waitress service and strong coffee.  You'll find fresh produce and imported products from Mexico.  5200 W. Oklahoma Ave., Milwaukee 53219 (414) 541-5200 www.elreyfoods.com

**Sasta Bazaar.**  An Indian grocer with good service, they cut your meat just like you want it.  You can get halal meat, even mutton and goat. They also have more varieties of rice than I could count, a colorful collection of spices, and curries in all temperatures, cookies, and a great juice selection. 708 W. Historic Mitchell St., Milwaukee 53204 (414) 672-7272

**Glorioso's Italian Market.** When you want authentic Italian products, this is the place.  The deli has a fantastic selection; so even if you don't need to do a big shopping order, try something new for lunch. 1011 E. Brady St., Milwaukee 53202  (414) 272-0540 www.gloriosos.com

**Pacific Produce.**  This is more of a mega Asian market.  I can't even tell you what some of the seafood is, but if you're an Asian chef, you will find whatever you need here.  This is one stop shopping.  Allow yourself plenty of time for the first visit so you can stroll the aisles.  5455 S. 27th St., Milwaukee 53221 (414) 308-1095

# 47. GET A BIRD'S EYE VIEW OF THE CITY

Milwaukee's skyline is still growing. According to Wikipedia, we have 115 high-rise buildings. The latest built was the new Potawatomi Casino Hotel in 2014. The highest is the **US Bank building** (at 601 feet), which does not have a public observation deck. It is usually open to the public during Doors Open Milwaukee, and there are often other tall buildings on the schedule as well: The **Gas Light Building, Hyatt Regency's Polaris Restaurant,** or the iconic **Allen Bradley Clock Tower.** www.doorsopenmilwaukee.org.

I'll list a few spaces here that are open more regularly to the public.

**Aurora St. Luke's Hospital.** Here you'll find an award winning rooftop garden, designed by Stano Landscaping. Take the elevator in the patient towers to the 8th floor. Called the hospital healing garden, it is approximately 14,000 square feet, including a 4,000 square foot glass conservatory for year round access to the garden's trees, shrubs, flowers and water features. The conservatory roof is covered in sedum, which helps contain rainwater. The sweeping view includes Miller Park, downtown Milwaukee and Lake Michigan. In fall, you can see the entire Menomonee Valley in full color. This is the view in the photo above. Open every day from 5 am- 9 pm. 2900 W. Oklahoma Ave., Milwaukee 53215

**Kilbourn Reservoir Park**. Take the stairs or the ramps to the top of this 35-acre park in Riverwest for stunning views of the city and lake. The Kilbourn reservoir used to be a water storage facility that held 21 million gallons of water. It was used until 2004, but then the tanks were demolished and removed. It's designated as a historic site and is a reminder of Milwaukee's first great public works project, the public water system. Don't let the cold weather keep you away. Some of the best winter views are from the top of this hill because there are no leaves on the trees. The backside of the hill is used for sledding. North Ave. at Humboldt.

**Kil@wat.** This won't get you very high off the ground, but if you're lucky enough to grab a seat at the window, you'll have the best view of Red Arrow Park's ice rink in winter, and of the intersection outside the Marcus Center. This is prime people watching! At Kilbourn and Water (thus the name) (414) 291-4793 http://www.kilawatcuisine.com

**Milwaukee Athletic Club.** With a rooftop bar open only during summer, you get a nice view of the downtown. This is the highest patio in the city. Host to the NEWaukee Koss Lunar music series, it's open on Friday evenings to Newaukee members and their guests. On a daily basis, it's a private club that gives members and hotel guests access. 758 N. Broadway, Milwaukee 53202 (414) 273-5080 www.macwi.org

**Pfister Hotel**. To see the beautifully lit city at night, have a drink at the rooftop bar Blu on the 23$^{rd}$ floor. Open Monday-Saturday with live music weekends from 8 pm-midnight. 424 E. Wisconsin Ave., Milwaukee 53202. www.thepfisterhotel.com

## 48. DO THE LAKEFRONT TRAIL

The paved trail that runs along Lake Michigan has some stunning views of sailboats, tall buildings, and the lake. The trail runs from the north end of town near the University of Wisconsin-Milwaukee through all the major lakefront tourist attractions and ends up south of the city in South Milwaukee. You can just take a walk and enjoy it, but if you are more adventurous, there are some other options.

**Milwaukee Bike and Skate Rental**. This shop in the heart of Veterans Park has been here for more than 20 years. They offer a variety of rentals. You can take a Segway tour for less than $50. You can use multi-person bicycles, and even rollerblades. It operates from Memorial Day through Labor Day, 10-7. 1500 N. Lincoln Memorial Dr., Milwaukee 53211 (414) 273-1343 www.milwbikeskaterental.com

**Bublr Bikes**. Look for the blue 3-speed bikes that come with a basket attached to the front to store your camera and other goods. The seats are adjustable. The gears make biking a breeze. Use your credit card to pay. Bike along the lakefront. Get the free B-Cycle Now app to find a Bublr bike anywhere in the network. www.bublrbikes.com

## 49. GET AN OAK LEAF DISCOVERY TOUR PASSPORT AND SEE MORE OF MILWAUKEE COUNTY PARKS

This is a new evolving program, but the idea is to get more people into the parks, and to make it as easy as possible to find your way between the 16 county parks along or near the 115-mile Oak Leaf Trail. Every year there is a new passport, complete with maps and stations where you can get stamps or secret words to write in your passport. Each page of the passport contains the name and address of the parks in each corridor. At the end of the summer, you validate the passport and can win prizes for participating. Some of the prizes are pretty awesome- like brand new bikes.

The real reward lies in spending some quality time outdoors and maybe discovering a few new places in and out of your neighborhood. You can do this alone or join rides that are organized by friends of the parks or through local bike stores. Now that we have Bublr bike kiosks (www.bublrbikes.com), there's really no excuse for you not to try a little biking, if you are able. If you have a smart phone, you can download the 'Milwaukee Bikes' app, which helps you navigate the trail.

The program runs from May through October. www.parkpeople.org

## 50. BE PART OF A MILWAUKEE EVENT AS A PARTICIPANT OR VOLUNTEER

The photo above is from one of the most original events I know about. It's called the Riverwest 24. It's a bike event with community ties. Quite an exercise in stamina, since you need to bike with your team for 24 hours, but it's also a chance to try a few new things. They have bonus checkpoints for community service, or sillier things like doing shots, getting a tattoo, and even shaving your head. People along the route bring out lawn chairs, appetizers, and even yard games. It truly is like nothing else you're likely to encounter.

We like to have fun in Milwaukee. It's even more fun if there are lots of people joining in the activity with us. There are way too many events to list here, but you can find some at www.visitmilwaukee.org/events or www.onmilwaukee.com/events and see what fits your personality best. Sign up. Show up. Make some friends. Have some fun!

# 51. STAND UP ON A PADDLEBOARD AT VETERAN'S PARK

**Wheel Fun Rentals** offers stand up paddleboards for rent by the hour ($12) at Veteran's Park. It really isn't that hard to balance, but it takes a few minutes to figure out how to paddle. Don't worry. If you get stuck, there are kayaks, pedal boats, and canoes. The staff is friendly and flexible.

Be sure to check their website and Groupon for discounts before you go to save a few bucks. There's no place to store anything on the boards, so leave your stuff in the car or on the shore. Open Memorial Day through Labor Day. 1400 N. Lincoln Memorial Dr., Milwaukee 53202 (414) 232-5027 www.wheelfunrentals.com/locations/milwaukee

**Milwaukee Power Yoga**. Feeling pretty sure of yourself? Try yoga on a paddleboard. Summer evenings once a week on Thursdays. Cost is $22. They say to bring a towel, change of clothes, and an open mind. Reserve in advance at their website. www.milwaukeepoweryoga.com

## 52. HAVE A PICNIC

What could possibly be better than good food and fresh air? Make a plan now to go somewhere and pack your picnic basket. If the refrigerator is empty, we have some great delis you can hit before you get there. Bring some friends and make some new memories. Not sure where to go? Try Lake Park, voted the best public park, where people have been having picnics since the early 1900s. 3233 E. Kenwood Blvd., Milwaukee 53211

**Jake's Deli**. People rave about the corned beef and pastrami. Try your sandwich grilled for extra effect. 1634 W. North Ave., Milwaukee 53205 (414) 562-1272 www.jakes-deli.com

**Koppa's Fulbeli Deli.** Just going inside is an experience. Taxidermy on the walls. Atari game playing while you wait. Every beverage known to man in their "Batcave" cooler. The deli boasts "world's best sandwiches" and has some interesting combos that are reasonable in price and overstuffed. My favorite is "Frukwine". You can pick up all the other snacks in the grocery aisles. 1940 N. Farwell Ave., Milwaukee 53202 (414) 273-1273 www.koppas.com

**Love Handle.** To the average diner, the menu might sound a bit unusual, but that's a good thing! It changes daily. Jump in and try something new like pickled beets. Sandwiches made on artisan bread from Wild Flour Bakery. Vegetarian options. This place makes Milwaukee interesting. 2215 E North Ave, Milwaukee (414) 271-1093

## 53. HONOR OUR VETERANS

Milwaukee is home to the 128th Air Refueling Wing, so we sometimes notice refueling aircraft flying overhead or see people in uniforms out for lunch. You'll also see military aircraft come in for the annual Lakefront Air & Water Show, held in June. If we're lucky, the Navy's Blue Angels or Air Force Thunderbirds put on a performance. We also have a population of veterans that show up for the Veteran's Day parade. You can always come out to either of these events and just say thanks to the veterans you meet.

Sadly, some of the homeless people you see on the streets of Milwaukee are veterans too. There are services available to help them, but you can help in a little more unconventional way by visiting these businesses, which serve them.

**Troop Café.** This not for profit café provides food service and hospitality training to veterans while serving delicious meals to the public. Meet Greg, the chef who trains them, and prepare to see passion in motion. Drop by for an affordable, healthy breakfast or lunch. 3430 W. Wisconsin Ave., Milwaukee 53208 (414) 763-7490 www.troopcafe.mke.com

**Milwaukee Homeless Veterans Services.** When you're doing some spring-cleaning, you might check with this organization to find out what's on their wish list. With an all-volunteer force, they provide services and household items to help get veterans back on their feet and set up in a Milwaukee home. You can call them to arrange for a pick-up. They also need volunteers, so if you have time to spare, you could help out. 5500 W. Greenfield Ave., Milwaukee 53214 www.yourneverhomeless.org

**Dryhootch.** Another not for profit organization that helps veterans and their families with a variety of reintegration issues, Dryhootch runs a couple of coffee houses for veterans, their families, and YOU. Enjoy a cup of coffee, tea, soda, and bakery items. Open Monday through Friday, this is an alcohol free/drug free zone. They also have a peer-mentoring program if you'd like to volunteer. 1030 E. Brady St., Milwaukee 53202 and 4801 W. National Ave., Milwaukee 53214 www.dryhootch.org

**USO of Wisconsin.** The USO organizes and sponsors events for active military families and veterans. Volunteer to help out with an event or spend some time helping traveling vets in the USO room at General Mitchell airport. www.uso.org/wisconsin/

**War Memorial Center.** Visit the center, which honors our veterans. All exhibits are free to the public during normal operating hours, but donations are welcome. 750 N. Lincoln Memorial, Milwaukee (414) 273-5533 www.warmemorialcenter.org

# 54. DO A STAYCATION AT A BOUTIQUE HOTEL

When you live in a city, you rarely decide to spend the night at a hotel. Why not change all that? See the city as a tourist sees it. Do the nightlife with no worries about driving. Dance the night away. Enjoy sleeping in. Go out for breakfast. Luckily for us, we have quite a few unique boutique hotels, each with a different theme. Most even welcome pets! Try one of these or discover your own favorite sleepover spot. Be sure to check for special packages that often include breakfast or other amenities.

**The Iron Horse Hotel.** Ranked #1 Milwaukee hotel on tripadvisor, it's hard to believe it was a warehouse. It's upscale. They welcome and pamper your dogs. Since this is just up the street from the Harley Davidson museum, motorcycle enthusiasts are encouraged to stay, with special racks in the rooms for your leather, a bike wash, and covered motorcycle parking. Each room has painted murals featuring local models. With spa amenities and onsite restaurants, you wouldn't really need to leave. 500 W. Florida St., Milwaukee 53204 (414) 374-4766 www.theironhorsehotel.com

**Hotel Metro.** Art deco design with eco friendly features, this hotel is listed as a historic hotel. The building was the first in Milwaukee to have central air. Now it has high tech amenities and room service...even for your dogs. Outdoor sun deck and cruiser bikes in summer. 411 E. Mason St., Milwaukee 53202 (414) 272-1937 www.hotelmetro.com

**Hilton Garden Inn Milwaukee Downtown.** This new hotel is in the restored Loyalty building, which is fantastic architecturally. They have gone to great lengths to preserve the original décor and added photographs of old trains from the Milwaukee Road. The floors are colorful and intricately pieced. 611 N. Broadway, Milwaukee 53202 (414) 271-6611 http://www.hiltongardeninnmilwaukeedowntown.com

**The Brewhouse Inn & Suites.** Imagine sleeping in a historic brewery, but with all the comforts. This ultra green hotel has gone to great lengths to be sustainable. The rooms have steampunk and Victorian styled décor...oh, and some huge shiny copper brewing kettles. Have a beer at the attached pub or walk down the street to Best Place. 1215 N. 10th St., Milwaukee 53205 (414) 810-3350 www.brewhousesuites.com

**The Pfister.** A Milwaukee icon, this hotel has been a prominent feature in our downtown since it opened in 1893. People stay here to be pampered. The interior is opulent with beautiful paintings and chandeliers. The staff is attentive and caters to any whim. The doormen greet you as you come back to the hotel from a fun day/night out. Pet friendly packages. 424 E. Wisconsin Ave., Milwaukee 53202 http://www.thepfisterhotel.com

**Aloft.** In the heart of the business district on the Milwaukee River, this modern hotel has comfortable rooms in a great location. Fitness center and pool. It's dog friendly. Close to restaurants and nightlife. You could even boat here and hook up at the dock next to the hotel. 1230 Old World Third St., Milwaukee 53212, (414) 226-0122 www.aloftmilwaukeedowntown.com

**Ambassador Hotel.** Another art deco hotel, which was recently completely restored. It is lovely inside and out. Liberace used to play on the piano here in the 1930s. The Beatles and JFK have been guests. The advantage to staying here is their shuttle service, so you only need to park once. 2308 W. Wisconsin Ave., Milwaukee 53233 (888) 322-3326 www.ambassadormilwaukee.com

**Milwaukee Athletic Club.** When it's all about location, this puts you in the heart of downtown with great workout facilities and pools too. During summer you can go to the highest patio in the city on the rooftop. They have valet parking and an evening shuttle for getting around the city. 758 N. Broadway, Milwaukee 53202 (414) 273-5080 www.macwi.org

## 55. TRY AN ETHNIC RESTAURANT

Our city's diversity pays off when you're looking for an interesting meal. Be a little adventurous when choosing a meal out. You can eat with chopsticks or even your fingers. I'll list a few that we've enjoyed, but feel free to explore the city and maybe you'll find something new. Most of these are probably considered "hole in the wall", but don't judge a restaurant by its storefront.

**Alem Ethiopian Village.** The photo above shows one of their combination plates. Everything is eaten with fingers so it's messy, but delicious. They do a popular vegan lunch buffet Tuesday through Friday. 307 E. Wisconsin Ave., Milwaukee 53202 (414) 224-5324 www.alem-ethiopianvillage.com

**Blue Star Café.** I have to mention this because it is delicious Somali food, and the owners are good friends of our family. I'm married to a Somali (disclaimer) My favorite dish is the chicken and rice. Be sure to ask for sambusa, a triangular fried appetizer filled with meat and veggies. 1619 N. Farwell Ave., Milwaukee 53221 (414) 273-9744

**El Senorial.** Authentic Mexican food that is cheap, fast, and tasty. Mariachi band and flowers for sale sometimes. 1901 S. 31st. St., Milwaukee 53215 (414) 385-9506

**Guanajuato.** Another delicious Mexican restaurant in a different part of town. Serving breakfast, lunch, and dinner at good prices. 2301 S. Howell Ave., Milwaukee 53207 (414) 482-2269

**Sake Tumi.** Asian, Korean BBQ, and fusion with a sushi bar. They do a comedy show dinner the first Saturday of each month. 714 N. Milwaukee St., Milwaukee 53202 (414) 224-SAKE www.sake-milwaukee.com

**Anmol Restaurant.** Indian/Pakistani cuisine. Start out with a mango lassi, if you've never had it. Food is not too spicy, and is made with halal meats, which comes from the grocer next door. No alcohol or pork dishes, true to Muslim tradition. 711 W. Historic Mitchell St., Milwaukee 53204 (414) 672-7878 www.anmolcuisines.com

**Stone Bowl.** Korean style hot stone bibimbop. This has all the traditional side dishes like kimchi. Featured are hot bowls filled with vegetables that continue to cook as you eat them. You can have other things added like tofu or beef. Very tasty, especially on a cold day. 1958 N. Farwell Ave., Milwaukee 53202 (414) 220-9111 www.stonebowlgrill.com

**Jow Nai Fouquet.** A small Thai restaurant with big city quality. Tom yum soup and crab rangoon are favorites, but every dish here is delicious. For the real adventure seeker, try the Thai iced tea or a bubble smoothie. 1978 N. Farwell Ave., Milwaukee 53202 (414) 270-1010 www.jownai.com

**Aladdin.** A large food stand in the Milwaukee Public Market featuring falafel, hummus, lentil soup, and a variety of Middle Eastern dishes. A healthy choice when you're in a hurry. 400 N. Water St., Milwaukee 53202 (414) 271-0400

**La Merenda.** For a wide variety of international small plates, this is a great place to come. Each menu item is labeled so you know the country of origin. You feel like you've traveled the world when you've eaten here. Make a reservation. 125 E. National Ave., Milwaukee 53204 (414) 389-0125 www.lamerenda125.com

**Mr. Perkins.** Soul food southern style. This little diner serves up heaping helpings of collard greens, fried chicken, okra, and corn bread. The catfish is a very popular dish. Sweet potato pie for dessert. Cash only. 2001 W. Atkinson Ave., Milwaukee WI 53209 (414) 447-6660

**Zarletti.** You'll believe you're in an authentic trattoria when you eat this Italian food in this cozy space. 741 N. Milwaukee St., Milwaukee 53202 (414) 225-0000 www.zarletti.net

**Zaffiro's Pizza.** The authentic Sicilian thin crust pizza recipe became the Milwaukee standard. This lovely family run café with red checked tables is just like being in Italy. 1724 N. Farwell Ave., Milwaukee 53202 (414) 289-8776 www.saffirospizza.com

**Mr. Sebass.** Authentic Peruvian dishes like ceviche, fried chicken with yucca and a variety of potatoes. 3427 W. National Ave., Milwaukee 53215 (414) 383-0300 www.mrsebass.com

## 56. EXPERIENCE SUMMERFEST

The world's largest outdoor summer music festival is all ours. It's uniquely Milwaukee. Over 11 days and 11 stages, you can see 800 acts. People come to see the hottest stars, and most of the shows are free with general admission. Whatever your taste in music, there's something for you.

In addition to the music, there are parades, rides, great food, cold beer, cooking demos, shopping, and a splash pad and entertainment for the kids. Each year brings new changes. It's always evolving and will celebrate 50 years in 2017. There's even a smartphone app for that!

From late June through early July, nearly 900,000 people will attend Summerfest. Make sure one of them is YOU!

Henry Maier Festival grounds. 200 N. Harbor, Milwaukee 53202 (414) 273-2680. www.summerfest.com

## 57. GO TO AN ETHNIC, CHURCH,
## OR STREET FESTIVAL

Summerfest isn't the only festival happening in Milwaukee. All summer long, you can find something every weekend. Maybe that's why Milwaukee has been called the "City of Festivals". OnMilwaukee has a complete listing of festivals www.onmilwaukee.com/myomc/festivals.

Most ethnic events are held at Maier Festival grounds, but be sure to check the venue. All of them add flavor to our city in special ways. The biggest and best festivals? I'd say choose Festa Italiana or Brady Street Festival. You're bound to have fun, eat some good food, and just be entertained. People watching is prime. Always check out the individual websites for ethnic festivals to see if there are admission deals.

## 58. RIDE IN A CARRIAGE

Sure you could walk around the city, but why not try something a little bit different? You can use human power or horse powered carriage. Both of these businesses are available for special occasions.

**Cream City Rickshaw.** Milwaukee's full service Pedi cab business doesn't have standard fares, but does trips for tips. If you appreciate getting a nontraditional lift around the city, tip generously. If you see an empty Pedi cab riding around, just flag them down or call to arrange more formal transportation. (414) 272-RIDE. www.creamcityrickshaw.com

**Milwaukee Coach & Carriage.** Make a reservation for a scenic ride through the city while the driver and horse do the work. You can always bring a carrot to "tip" the horse. Rides start at 6 on weekdays and 5 on weekends. Meet your carriage at the Pfister, Hyatt, and Intercontinental hotels. 228 E. National Ave., Milwaukee 53204 (414) 272-6873 www.milwaukeecarriage.com

## 59. GO FISHING

With three rivers, a lake, and many stocked park lagoons, you're bound to find some good fishing in Milwaukee. The Menomonee River was named one of the country's top urban fisheries by Field & Stream magazine. Salmon travel through the Milwaukee River in fall through Estabrook and Kletzsch parks. McKinley Marina is good for dock fishing if you go to the inlet across from Colectivo at the Lake.

All adults need a valid fishing license. You can purchase a license at the Milwaukee Natural Resources Department. 2300 N. Martin Luther King Dr., Milwaukee or order online at www.takemefishing.org. That website has everything you will probably need to know about fishing. Additional stamps are needed for Lake Michigan salmon and brown trout.

You can use fishing gear at any of the three **Urban Ecology Centers** for free if you're a member. It costs $35 per person or $45 per family annually and you'll have access to all the recreation equipment. All the poles come with a bobber, sinker, and hook. You just need to bring the bait or lures. www.urbanecologycenter.org

If you're more interested in fishing on Lake Michigan, you can book a charter boat at McKinley Marina. There are a number of boats available, but I used **Ray's the Limit Charters.** It was a great experience! Spend a half or full day with Captain Andy. It was like hanging out with a good friend. The best part? He helps you as much as you request- including cleaning the fish. You only pay if you catch fish! 1450 N. Lincoln Memorial Dr., Milwaukee 53202 (414) 379-5820 www.raysthelimit.com

## 60. SHARE SOME BAKERY

Bakeries are disappearing from our Main streets and being replaced by specialty shops that serve doughnuts, bagels, pastries, and cupcakes. That's not necessarily a bad thing. When you're ready to indulge, I suggest taking a friend, or picking up a box to bring with you to the office or the park. Sharing bakery should become a Milwaukee tradition! Here are a few of my favorite spots when you're in the mood.

**North Shore Boulangerie**. This takes me right back to Alsace, France. When I need fresh almond croissants or a quiche, this is the place. Everything is fresh and buttery, which means there will be crumbs. You won't be able to hide that you've been here! Summer outdoor seating. The café is also cozy indoors. 4401 N. Oakland Ave., Shorewood 53211 (414) 963-2153 www.northshoreboulangerie.com

**Classy Girl Cupcakes**. We've tasted a lot of cupcakes, and these take the cake, so to speak. Just the right texture and made with real ingredients like fresh butter, they come in a variety of flavors. Anything with chocolate is delicious! 825 N. Jefferson St., Milwaukee 53202 (414) 270-1877 www.classygirlcupcakes.com

**Holey Moley Doughnuts**. This takes doughnuts to a whole new level. They specialize in gourmet doughnuts with flavors like peanut butter and bacon. You never know what they'll be cooking up. 316 N. Milwaukee St., Milwaukee 53202 (414) 308-1616 www.holeymoleydoughnuts.com

**National Bakery and Deli.** Consistently voted #1. A full service bakery with all the traditional baked goods one would expect, but they add fun twists to things as well. I love the cookies- the icing is so delicious.

Watch for themes celebrating local events and seasons- pig cookies and cream puffs during the fair, baseball cookies during the baseball season. You'll want to stop in just to see the seasonal items. Try the jelly filled paczkis, when you are off your diet. They have multiple locations, but the Milwaukee store is on the east side at 3200 S. 16th St., Milwaukee 53215 (414) 672-1620 www.nationalbakery.com

**Peter Sciortino's Bakery**. Italian pastries and cookies that melt in your mouth. When I buy these, I have to put them in the trunk while I drive home or I'd eat the whole box! 1101 East Brady St., Milwaukee 53202 (414) 272-4623 www.petersciortinosbakery.com

**Wild Flour Bakery.** Have you ever tasted really good artisan bread but wanted it in a bagel? They do that here. Some unusual combinations like Five Cheese and Jalapeno Cheese, as well as muffins and other treats. They have multiple locations but this is the bake house. 2800 W. Lincoln Ave., Milwaukee 53215 (414) 831-1692 www.wildflour.net

**Honeypie Café**. Known to use local ingredients and keep everything as fresh as possible, this café has nationally acclaimed pies. Travel & Leisure wrote about their cheddar bacon apple pie, but everything will surely satisfy. 2643 S. Kinnickinnic Ave., Milwaukee 53207 (414) 489-PIES www.honeypiecafe.com

**Colectivo Coffee.** Fantastic baked goods here, but some of the best muffins and bagels you'll find anywhere with all kinds of crunchy goodness, so you will believe they are healthy for you. Multiple locations but try the lakefront if weather is nice. This café is built into the restored Milwaukee River Flushing Station. 1701 N. Lincoln Memorial Dr., 53202 (414) 223-4551 www.colectivo.com

**Bus Stop Coffee Shop**. In the heart of Milwaukee's Washington Park neighborhood, what makes this unusual is the way in which they serve the community. You will often find the owners chatting up the young skateboarders who live in the neighborhood. Their motto; "Transforming the neighborhood, one cookie at a time!" I'd try the lemon squares, but everything here is delicious. There is also a photography studio next door. Take a peek! 4424 W. Lisbon Ave., Milwaukee 53208 (414) 939-8765 www.bustopcoffeeshop.com

**Amaranth Bakery & Cafe**. Tough to choose a favorite, but the scones, rugelach, and croissants are a good starting point. Artisan style baked goods using organic ingredients. Later in the day, the sandwiches and soups are great too. 3329 W. Lisbon Ave., Milwaukee 53208 (414) 934-0587

**Simma's Bakery**. Cheesecake is the highlight here, though they do have pastries too. The chocolate ganache covered desserts are to die for. Just looking the photos on their website will make you salivate. 817 N. 68th St., Wauwatosa, 53213 (414) 257-0998 www.simmasbakery.com

## 61. ATTEND A BOOKSTORE EVENT

**Boswell Book Company** is an independent bookseller in Milwaukee, and they already know pretty much everything you'll ever want to know about books and authors. Every week, authors from all over the world vie for a spot to hold talks, do readings, or share stories. Local writers launch their first books here. The crew at Boswell, headed by Daniel Goldin, partner with local businesses to offer fine arts previews and tasty foods. They even bring authors to schools and libraries. It's fun to attend one of these events and meet your favorite authors. There's something for every age and interest. Check out the coming events page or subscribe to the newsletter. 2559 N. Downer Ave., Milwaukee 53211 (414) 332-1181 www.boswellindiebound.com

## 62. TAKE A YOGA CLASS

Milwaukee has become a regular yoga mecca. You can find a class of many different varieties just about any day of the week, in every neighborhood. During the summer you can find drop in classes at Bradford Beach, Villa Terrace, Cathedral Square Park, Boerner Botanical Gardens, Bayshore Town Center, Alice's Garden, and some of the public libraries. Lake Park has a weekly session all year round. If you're not sure what kind of yoga class you might enjoy, check for local deals at www.groupon.com. These usually allow you to take a class at a reduced price. I've listed a few places that show the variety Milwaukee offers.

**Milwaukee Power Yoga**. Try the hot vinyasa yoga studio where classes combine heat, music, breath and movement. They also lead the stand up paddleboard classes at Veterans Park in summer. 1824 N. Farwell Ave., Milwaukee 53202 (414) 731-1550 www.milwaukeepoweryoga.com

**Invivo**. The location of this total wellness center makes it a real retreat. You can look over the Milwaukee River from the sunlit studio or the rooftop. 2060 N. Humboldt Ave., Milwaukee 53212 (414) 265-5606 www.invivowellness.com

**Yoga Rocks the Park.** During summer, there are outdoor yoga sessions at the base of the grand staircase at Lake Park every Sunday at 9:30. Bring your own mat and dress in layers. Guest instructors are paired with musicians for a total experience. www.yogarocksthepark.com/Milwaukee

**Zenzen Yoga Arts.** Milwaukee's first aerial yoga studio, if you're ready for something different. Try the Saturday morning play session for beginners. The stretching is good for all ages. 900 S. 5th St., #305, Milwaukee 53204 (414) 973-9642 www.zenzenyogaarts.com

## 63. TRY THE MILWAUKEE GEOCACHING TOUR

Geocaching is a modern day treasure hunt where you get clues and coordinates to find puzzles, great views, or little boxes with prizes inside. This is a great way to discover Milwaukee's neighborhoods while getting some exercise. There are 15 different caches or hidden treasures spread across the city. You can download a passport and do additional challenges to find code words. Find the geotour and passport link at www.visitmilwaukee.org/geocache

If you are new to geocaching, you'll need a GPS device or a smartphone to find them. Get an account and learn more about geocaching in general at www.geocaching.com.

## 64. FLY A KITE

With our close proximity to Lake Michigan, kite flying is easy because we get wind near the shoreline. You can get a kite up anywhere along the lakefront, but **Veteran's Park** is the most popular.

There are kite festivals held at Veteran's Park a few times each year where expert teams bring in large kites and sport kites. You can sometimes see more than 500 kites aloft during the grand launch. Maybe yours will be one of them!

**Gift of Wings**, located inside the park, sells a variety of kites if you don't have one of your own. 1300 N. Lincoln Memorial Dr., Milwaukee 53202 (414) 273-5483 www.giftofwings.com

**Art Smart's Dart Mart** is another place to find a selection of kites. This is a unique spot to find all kinds of fun stuff for playing outdoors. 1695 N. Humboldt, Milwaukee 53202 (414) 273-3278 www.jugglingsupplies.net

## 65. RIDE A TROLLEY

This may be the best use of $1 that you'll ever find. Look for a trolley stop around the city, pay $1 when you board, and sit back for the next 40 minutes seeing the sights narrated by the driver. Even if you think you know the city, you're bound to learn something new.

You can get off the trolley to explore museums, get something to eat, or go to an event, but you will have to pay to get onboard again. Trolleys run Thursday through Saturday all summer long and come every 20 minutes.

Download a map at their website, or stand at one of these intersections. www.milwaukeedowntown.com/getting-around/milwaukee-trolley-loop/

4th & Michigan
3rd & Highland
Wells & Jefferson
Milwaukee Art Museum
Mason & Jefferson
Water & St. Paul

## 66. EAT SOMETHING ON A STICK
## AT WISCONSIN STATE FAIR

It used to be popular for people to go to the Wisconsin State Fair just to see the livestock and vie for ribbons for homegrown veggies. You can still do that, but state fair has certainly evolved! Now you can go for a ride at the midway, see the latest in gadgets, and eat your way through the park. Everyone probably knows we have tasty cream puffs. We eat more than 400,000 of them every year! There is also a stick culture. People like to eat and walk, so there are more than 150 choices of food on a stick. Saz's ribs sold nearly 6000 bacon wrapped cherry wood smoked pork belly on a stick in 2014. What will you try? There are food lists on two-smartphone apps-DUN and WISCONSIN STATE FAIR. Wisconsin State Fair Park, 640 S. 84th St., West Allis, 53214 (800) 884-FAIR www.wistatefair.com

## 67. HAVE FUN WITH DOGS

Milwaukee was voted as one of the most dog friendly cities. And why not? We have hotels that cater to pooches with room service! There are plenty of restaurants and coffee shops that welcome them on the patio. Some even provide snacks and water dishes. You don't need to own a dog to have some fun with them. There are plenty of spots where you can get your dog fix! Check out one of these fun events or places.

**ROMP.** If you are a dog owner, you'll want to know about Residents for Off-leash Milwaukee Parks. This is the place to find out about dog parks and dog events. www.milwaukeedogparks.org

**Wisconsin Humane Society.** They are always looking for volunteers. If you have some extra time and enjoy animals, fill out a volunteer form at their website. 4500 W. Wisconsin Ave., Milwaukee 53208 (414) 264-6257 www.wihumane.org

**Pug Fest.** A fundraiser to benefit pug rescues, this is the largest of its kind in the US! Held every May at the Milwaukee County Indoor Sports Complex. The pugs in costumes are the best part, but they also have pug races, silent auctions, and K-9 demonstrations with the County Sheriff's dogs.

**Doggie Dip.** This event, over Labor Day weekend, signals the end of the summer outdoor pool season when dogs are invited to swim at Cool Waters Aquatic Center. 2028 S. 124th St., West Allis 53227

**Zoom Room.** This is a dog-training center with a gym (above) you can rent out privately by the half hour to work with your dog. They also host doggie socials. 1701 N. Humboldt Ave., Milwaukee 53202 (414) 220-9202 www.zoomroomonline.com

**Nourri Doggy Dining.** Talk about pampered pooches…this restaurant has a special menu for dogs! Every Wednesday and Saturday evening during summer (on the patio), owners can dine with their pets. The restaurant serves small plates for humans. 5901 W. Vliet St., Milwaukee 53208 (414) 727-0860

**Brady Street.** You just have to walk through this neighborhood to know it is dog friendly. Water dishes are set out routinely, and I've even some doggie poetry during the art festival. They host a pet parade every October. Be sure to bring your camera for the costumes! You can enter the Human Bark contest, if that's your special talent. www.bradystreet.org

**Great Lakes Pet Expo**. In winter, State Fair Park becomes a haven for pet lovers for a day. This unique event raises money for animals in need, and features a variety of animals along with dogs. 8200 W. Greenfield Ave., Milwaukee www.petexpomilwaukee.com

**Pet Fest**. Milwaukee has a festival for everyone, and now for pets as well. In September, the Henry Maier Festival Park is open to people with their pets for a day. It's free with free parking. You'll see dock diving, nutritional seminars, and family focused games. You won't want to miss the people/pet look-alike contest. Of course, there's music and food too. 200 N. Harbor Dr., Milwaukee (920) 350-FEST www.petfestmke.com

**Barktoberfest.** What better place to celebrate Oktoberfest with a dog than a beer garden? Pack a picnic basket and bring your dog with you to Estabrook Park in fall for a day. An agility course is part of the fun. There are pet costume contests, live music, and a commemorative glass beer mug. 4610 Estabrook Pkwy., Milwaukee 53211

# 68. LEARN MORE ABOUT HISTORIC MILWAUKEE'S BUILDINGS

Have you been inside our city hall (shown above)? Did you know that in 1895 it was listed as the tallest building in the US?

Milwaukee has a wide variety of architectural delights. Here old buildings are repurposed rather than destroyed. Just go inside any of the historic buildings along or near Wisconsin Avenue and you'll be impressed. Many are open to the public every day- Federal Courthouse & Federal Office Building, Mackie Building, and the Hilton Garden Inn.

For the past few years, a small group in Milwaukee has made a huge impact. In 2010, they decided to see how many businesses would open their doors for a September weekend at no cost to the public. The event was called Doors Open Milwaukee. www.doorsopenmilwaukee.org

**Historic Milwaukee, Inc.,** plans the now annual event that has been growing in size. If you're able to walk through one of the buildings or take a special tour during that fall weekend, you're bound to learn something and have a good time doing it. They also lead neighborhood-walking tours year round, for a small fee. Passionate volunteers tell stories about the past and present history of the buildings and people of Milwaukee.

You can sign up for tours (and save $$ if you become a member) at their website. They also need volunteers for the Doors Open Milwaukee event, so if you have time, let them know. Take a tour that interests you. Mitchell Building, 207 E. Michigan St., Suite 406, Milwaukee 53202 (414) 277-7795 www.historicmilwaukee.org

## 69. KAYAK THE MILWAUKEE RIVERS

You haven't truly experienced Milwaukee until you've seen it from the river. We have the **Milwaukee Urban Water Trail**, which is a canoe and kayak route through the urban portions of the Milwaukee, Menomonee, and Kinnickinnic Rivers, with more than 25 miles of paddling. You can download a map at www.mkeriverkeeper.org if you have your own kayak. It tells you where you can launch and shows portage spots. Restaurants are also clearly marked.

**Milwaukee Kayak Company** lets you see the Milwaukee Rivers from the seat of a kayak. They have single or tandem kayaks, as well as canoes and standup paddleboards. Rentals are available Tuesday through Sunday. Kayaking is easy to learn. Safety gear and a paddle are included in the rental fee. If you're still nervous, sign up for one of the guided paddles sessions. You can make an advance reservation. There are several places to dock along restaurants if you want to make a day of it. 318 S. Water St., Milwaukee 53204 (414) 301-2240 www.milwaukeekayak.com

**Milwaukee River History Tour.** Combine history and kayaking with a three hour tour that includes equipment and commentary. No experience necessary. (262) 895-2008 www.sherrikayaks.com

**Urban Ecology Center.** Become a member. Take a 30-minute water safety course. Then use of kayaks is free. They also offer guided paddling trips. Riverside Park, 1500 E. Park Pl., Milwaukee 53211 (414) 964-8505 www.urbanecologycenter.org

## 70. TAKE A COOKING CLASS

Have you always wanted to learn to cook something you've tasted in a restaurant? We have a lot of talented chefs in Milwaukee, and some teach classes at the **Milwaukee Public Market**. This is an open space on the second floor of the market. You can see the upcoming events online and sign up either at the website or by phone.

You'll sit and watch a demonstration with other students, then have the opportunity to do it yourself with the supervision of a chef. The best part…you get to eat whatever you make! You can even suggest a class or ask questions of a chef. 400 N. Water St., Milwaukee 53202 (414) 336-1111 www.milwaukeepublicmarket.org/classes.html

Of course, there are other locations where you'll find cooking classes too: libraries, park and recreation programs, and restaurants. Find one that you'll enjoy.

# 71. MAKE FRIENDS AT A BEER GARDEN

In recent years, beer gardens are making a big impact on park revenues in Milwaukee. They are family friendly and a great gathering place for people to socialize outdoors in the parks. Some are permanently set up for summer, but we also have a traveling beer garden that rotates through the parks. Expect more of these in the future. Find your favorite- they are each unique. All of them serve beer, soft drinks, and food- think sausages and pretzels with creamy mustard. You will usually find live music on weekends (usually polka music). Bring your own glass, or borrow/buy one of theirs. You are encouraged to bring a picnic basket too. For a full schedule of beer gardens in Milwaukee county parks, you can check the website. http://county.milwaukee.gov/Parks/BeerGardens

**Traveling Beer Garden.** Featuring Sprecher's drinks, this converted fire truck brings everything it needs to make the park a party. Be sure to try the root beer floats and the cheesy popcorn. www.sprecherbrewery.com

**The Landing at Hoyt Park.** Operated by Friends of Hoyt Park and pool, it has nice views of the Menomonee River Parkway. The menu changes here but you can get a variety of imported and local brews, along with wine. 1800 Swan Blvd, Wauwatosa 53226 (414) 302-9160 www.friendsofhoytpark.org/main/thelanding

**Hubbard Park Lodge Beer Garden**. If you love the lodge, you'll love the beer garden. Set on the river in scenic Hubbard Park, you can share a picnic table and try a variety of imported and domestic brews, as well as Bota and Wollersheim wines. 3865 N. Morris Blvd., Shorewood www.hubbardparkbeergarden.com

**Estabrook Beer Garden.** This was the first truly public beer garden in America in nearly 100 years. Its popularity is colossal, meaning that parking is difficult to find on a weekend. Modeled after beer gardens found in Munich, Germany, it's a great place to enjoy nature with a cold brew. Beers here are imported from Munich Hofbrauhaus. 4600 Estabrook Dr., Milwaukee 53217 www.oldgermanbeerhall.com

**Humboldt Park Beer Garden.** Operated by St. Francis Brewing Company, this is a nice shady location with a horseshoe pit. You'll find it located near the pavilion. Try the cheese soup served in a bread bowl, or the delicious pretzel rolls. They even have a vegetarian frankfurter. You'll find beer, wine, and maple root beer. 3000 S. Howell Ave, Milwaukee 53207 (414) 257-8005 www.stfrancisbrewery.com/SFB.php

# 72. TAKE A HIKE

With so many beautiful parks in Milwaukee, it's no surprise that people like to get out into nature. My favorite hike is at Grant Park, through the beautiful Seven Bridges Trail. You can hear the leaves rustle as the wind blows through the creek bed down to the lake. Often you can find deer hiding behind the trees. It's a picture perfect setting.

When you want to find a place to hike, go to the Milwaukee Park People website. This nonprofit group supports the county parks through education, fundraising, and park improvements. They have nearly 30 different downloadable files for day hikes, created by Brian Russart, the Milwaukee County Parks Natural Areas Coordinator, and his crew. http://www.parkpeoplemke.org/hiking-trails-milwaukee-county-parks

If 12 miles through what used to be the industrial heart of the city is more appealing, hike the **Hank Aaron trail**. This rail to trail project brings you from the lakefront at Discovery World through Three Bridges Park, and out to Miller Park. You'll see a big chunk of the Menomonee Valley this way. www.hankaaronstatetrail.org

**Schlitz Audubon Nature Center.** With six miles of hiking trails along the lake, around ponds, and through hills, it's a scenic place to enjoy nature. Climb the 60-foot high tower for a little extra exercise and a great view. Admission fee. 1111 E. Brown Deer Rd., Milwaukee 53217 (414) 352-2880 http://www.sanc.org

**Havenwoods State Forest** has just over six miles of trails that offer views of woods, meadows, and wetlands. Some are pet friendly. Free. 6141 N. Hopkins St., Milwaukee 53209 (414) 527-0232 www.dnr.wi.gov

**Brew City Safari** has free hiking tours led by a local who loves to hike, takes photos, and knows a lot about Milwaukee. Find the Facebook page for upcoming hikes or email brewcitysafari@gmail.com.

## 73. HAVE A SPA DAY

Who doesn't need a bit of pampering? We have just the ticket for those tired shoulders or unruly hair. There is something for every price range-just check Groupon for deals in our area on haircuts and massages. For the total package or a fun day out, here are a couple of spas at both ends of the spectrum, which you won't find on Groupon.

**The Pfister Well Spa + Salon.** This exquisite place takes the entire spa experience to a whole new level. But who wouldn't expect this of the Pfister? They have treatment rooms with private showers, heated floors, and tables with adjustable temperature. All massage includes aromatherapy. Try the hammam steam shower, and kick it up a notch by applying rhassoul mud over your entire body. Maybe a remineralizing hydrotherapy bath is what your aching muscles and mind need. Don't forget manicures, pedicures, facials, and hair. Believe me when I say they can do it all. 424 E. Wisconsin Ave., Milwaukee 53202 (414) 277-9207 www.pfisterwellspa.com

**The Institute of Beauty of Wellness. Aveda Beauty School.** Consider this your civic duty. Go let the students work magic on your body. You can do any spa service: massage, haircuts, manicure, pedicure, waxing, make-up. They need people to help them perfect their craft and sometimes they will do it for free, so check the blog/website for details. 327 E. St. Paul Ave., Milwaukee 53202 (414) 227-2889 www.institutebw.com

## 74. SEE STARS

The **Manfred Olson Planetarium** is located on the UWM campus, but is open to the public for a variety of interesting astronomy programs. For $3 you can learn about some skyward topic nearly every Friday night. The topic changes every 4-6 weeks. They also have free astrobreaks, short planetarium shows, on Wednesdays during the lunch hour. If you really want to see the stars, show up for FREE stargazing with high-powered telescopes, on the observing deck of the physics building. They usually offer this after dark a couple of times per month and for special lunar events. UWM Physics building, 1900 E. Kenwood Blvd., Milwaukee 53211 (414) 229-4961 www.uwm.edu/planetarium

# 75. TRY A MEATLESS MEAL

There was a time when a vegetarian had limited options for dining out in Milwaukee, but that sure isn't the norm now. Going meatless at least once a week is good advice to save money and cut down on fat in your diet. Plenty of restaurants and grocery stores offer good fare. Choose from the list below or find your own favorite spot. Ethnic restaurants that serve Indian, Pakistani, and Mediterranean are also good bets for some tasty vegetarian options.

All of these places offer meat dishes too, just in case you need to cater to a mixed dining group.

**Comet Café.** Since being featured on several TV shows, this place gets a lot of business. If you don't mind a few calories, the mac n cheese is to die for. In fact, there's lots of comfort food. The veggie sausage is something you probably haven't tried elsewhere. How about a vegan pita or a walnut burger? They host special events like Pie Spin (a live DJ and free pie.) 1947 N. Farwell Ave., Milwaukee 53202 (414) 273-7677 www.thecometcafe.com

**Wolf Peach**. Known for using fresh local ingredients, many from their own farm, this is an excellent place for anyone wanting a healthy and tasty meal. It's a good idea to look around the restaurant and see what others are having- then point and say, "I'll have what she's having", as each dish is prepared for the season.  Outdoor seating is the best. 1818 N. Hubbard St., Milwaukee 53212 (414) 374-8480 www.wolf-peach.com

**Meritage.** This is fine dining in a casual, intimate setting.  The menu and healthy food choices change frequently depending on what the supplying local farmers have to offer.  Most people are impressed with the high quality for a lower cost than you'd expect. They only serve dinner. 5921 W. Vliet St., Milwaukee 53208 (414) 479-0620 www.meritage.us

**Beans & Barley.** Not only do they have veggie options, but also you can get gluten free products. The menu has lots of healthy choices.  They make smoothies/juices to order. Portions are large and appetizing. 1901 E. North Ave., Milwaukee 53202 www.beansandbarley.com

**Riverwest Co-op & Café.** I love supporting this place because friendly volunteers man it.  You can buy organic options at the grocery part without wearing yourself out in a large space. The vegan tamales are highly recommended, but everything is veggie friendly and made fresh. Reasonable prices. 733 E. Clarke St., Milwaukee 53212 (414) 264-7933 www.riverwestcoop.org

**The Green Kitchen.**  At the Milwaukee Public Market, you can get a shot of wheat grass in your smoothie or juice and order up a healthy salad or sandwich.  You can see all the ingredients, which makes it easier to decide. There's always a line for a reason. The eating space is on the second floor, or you can carry out. 400 N. Water St., Milwaukee 53202 www.greenkitchenmke.com

**Café Corazon.** This is a great place, which can be crowded, so you may have to wait for a table. The best option is to go here in summer when you can ride your bike using the adjacent Beerline trail. Then you can get a seat on the patio.  Service is very quick.  The food is Mexican but the chef has a few twists that work magic with the vegetables.  I had the best salad of my life here.   31329 N. Bremen St., Milwaukee 53212 (414) 810-3941 www.corazonmilwaukee.com

**Sanford Restaurant.**  Though not really advertised as a vegetarian restaurant, the chef will make any dish to meet your needs.  This has been rated the #1 restaurant in Milwaukee for years.  It's legendary, but pricy, so when you want to impress your dinner date and be dazzled, this is the place to go. Try the fixed price exploration menu or surprise tasting menu. Make a reservation. 1547 N. Jackson St., Milwaukee 53202 (414) 276-9608 www.sanfordrestaurant.com

## 76. SEE THE FALL COLORS AT HOLY HILL BASILICA IN HUBERTUS

When leaves start to turn colors, the place to be is at Holy Hill. It's just a short drive from Milwaukee and takes you through some scenic wooded roadways. At the Basilica, you're on one of the highest points around so you can see all the way back to the city of Milwaukee on a clear day. If the tower is open, you have to attempt the 198 steps to the top. It's a long haul, but oh, so worth it! Before you is a palette of every shade of color as you look over the kettle moraine.

The church itself is also quite beautiful and when the bells ring, they are clear and true. Take the tour if you have time or schedule your visit around the mass. You can grab a bite to eat at the café near the parking lot. Be sure to save room for the homemade pies. When you're ready to drive back to the city, I recommend taking the south entrance via St. Augustine Road, which is a Wisconsin Rustic Road. 1525 Carmel Rd., Hubertus, 53033 (262) 628-1863 www.holyhill.com

# 77. HAVE A LAUGH AT A COMEDY SHOW

Laughter is good for the soul, so why not have a few laughs. We have a variety of fun places that will surely tickle your funny bone.

**Dinner Detective.** This comedy dinner show plays weekends at the Hyatt Regency. You never know who did it- could be that guy sitting next to you! 333 W. Kilbourn Ave., Milwaukee 53203. (414) 276-1234 www.thedinnerdetective.com/sites/milwaukee

**Murder Mystery Co.** Rock Bottom Brewery's interactive show. You work with a team interrogating suspects, gathering clues, and maybe crack the case. 740 N. Plankinton Ave., #1 Milwaukee (888) 643-2583 www.grimprov.com

**Comedy Sportz.** Interactive shows for all ages. There's a referee and two teams of players competing in improvisation games. Lots of fun. Full bar and restaurant. 420 S. First St., Milwaukee 53202 (414) 272-8888 www.comedysportzmilwaukee.com

**Comedy Café.** Nationally recognized comedians, and an open mic competition once a month. 615 E. Brady St., Milwaukee 53202 (414) 271-JOKE www.milwaukeescomedycafe.com

**Jokerz Comedy Club.** Order off their extensive menu while you laugh at the latest and greatest talent. They also have nationally recognized comedians. 11400 W. Silver Spring Rd., Milwaukee 53225 (414) 758-5101 www.jokerzcomedyclub.com

**Hamburger Mary's.** This is a burger joint that has Dining with the Divas, a funny show featuring drag queens. It's best to reserve a spot because seating is limited. 2130 S. Kinnickinnic Ave., Milwaukee 53207 (414) 988-9324 www.hamburgermarys.com/mke

# 78. DO THE STAIRS AT ATWATER BEACH

Known as the "killer stairs" because of how many there are and how steep they are, this is the fitness mecca of college students wanting to stay in shape. There is also a ramp, but try the stairs if you are able. You'll be rewarded with views of the lake from a beach hidden to most passersby. There's also a nice playground at the bottom with some unusual play toys designed for adults as well as kids. Look for the flagpole at street level, and the stairs are just below. 3920 N. Murray Ave., Shorewood 53211

## 79. GET A PHOTO WITH THE BRONZE FONZ
## AT THE RIVERWALK

Milwaukee's riverwalk is a fun place to stroll no matter what the weather. You'll see kayaks and boats passing by in summer. There are ducks and geese waddling across frozen snow in winter. Stop for a beverage on a patio or find a meal. Enjoy the artwork. Don't leave without taking a photo with the "Bronze Fonz", fashioned after the Happy Days character, Fonzie. Sometimes people dress him up with hats or scarves. His hands can hold a sign wishing someone a "Happy Birthday" or "Merry Christmas". Make your photo unique, even if it's a selfie. It will remind you of Milwaukee. 100 E. Wells St., Milwaukee 53202

# 80. BUY A LOCALLY MADE GIFT FOR SOMEONE SPECIAL

We're a city with a lot of local talent! Once you had to wait for an event to buy handmade Milwaukee items. Recently a few storefronts have opened that sell artisan-made goods year-round. Help support our local artists by buying local when you can.

**The Brass Rooster.** This shop makes amazing hats. You can even have one custom made. When you want quality and are willing to pay the price, this is a great place to go. 2250 S. Kinnickinnic Ave., Milwaukee 53207 (414) 988-5222

**Hometown Established**. A general store, with a large inviting space, focused on home-goods and handcrafted items all made by local artisans. The owner is warm and welcoming. This shop has baskets, soap, t-shirts, handcrafted rings, baby items, watercolor prints, and so much more. There's a rotating art gallery. You'll even find a water dish outside for your dog. Ask about classes. 130 W. Mineral St., Milwaukee 53204 (414) 416-0425 www.facebook.com/hometownestablished.generalstore

**The Waxwing.** A cute consignment shop featuring 90 artists packing in a lot of great gift ideas, you're likely to find something for everyone. Milwaukee Home is featured here, along with jewelry, baby items, bags, paintings, and even pottery. 4415 N. Oakland Ave., Shorewood, 53211 www.thewaxwing.com

**Our Daily Salt.** This is a woodcutting studio started by Chef Felisha Wild (above). When you walk in, the store's friendly dog will likely welcome you. You can smell wood from the workshop and see bowls being formed through the large glass windows. There are other artists' wares being sold in cases and displayed all over the storefront as well. You'll find unusual jewelry, cutting boards, kitchen tools, quilted fabric hangings, and furniture...just to name a few. 3519 W. National Ave., Milwaukee 53215 (414) 671-9453 www.ourdailysalt.com

**Barcelona Artful Living.** This corner store packs in a wide variety of locally made gifts. You can find doggie collars, leather bags, jewelry, scarves, pottery and repurposed furniture. In fact, if you're up to doing some refinishing of your own, pick up a can of Annie Sloan's chalk paint here and make that stuff in the garage attic new again. This is the regional supplier for that brand of paint. 5827 W. Vliet St., Milwaukee 53208 (414) 345-7494 www.barcelonatosa.com

**The Urban Milwaukee Store.** The store that promotes Milwaukee, and features puzzles, photos and paintings of Milwaukee landmarks. You can find a number of the historic Milwaukee book series. For the T-shirt lover, there's an entire wall of selections. 755 N. Milwaukee St., Milwaukee 53202 www.urbanmilwaukee.com/urban-milwaukee-the-store/

**Sparrow Collective.** Clothes, jewelry, art, cards with a Milwaukee theme, and handmade soap are only a few of the items in this eclectic mix. It's difficult to walk out empty handed. The designers are not all from Milwaukee, but there are plenty of locally made items. 2224 S. Kinnickinnic Ave., Milwaukee 53207 www.sparrowcollective.com

**Maker Market.** Colectivo Bay View hosts tables where handmade things are offered for sale by the local artisans who make them. It's the first Sunday of each month May-September. 2301 S. Kinnickinnic Ave., Milwaukee 53207 (414) 744-6117 www.colectivo.com

# 81. MAKE A SPLASH AT A WATERPARK

Milwaukee has four family-friendly aquatic centers open during the summer. For a reasonable price, you can have fun all day and stay cool riding the slides or floating the lazy river. You can bring your own food or buy something from the snack bars. Milwaukee County Parks maintains and staffs these. There's a hotline for more information that covers all four centers. (414) 257-8098
http://county.milwaukee.gov/FamilyWaterParks17755.htm

**Cool Waters.** Greenfield Park, 2028 S. 124th St., West Allis 53227
**David F. Schulz Aquatic Center**. Lincoln Park, 1301 W. Hampton Ave., Milwaukee 53209
**Pelican Cove.** Kosciuszko Park, 2201 S. 7th St., Milwaukee 53215
**Tosa Pool.** Hoyt Park, 1800 N. Swan Blvd, Wauwatosa 53226

## 82. LEARN ABOUT THE GREAT LAKES AT DISCOVERY WORLD

**Discovery World** is the lakefront science and technology center, packed with lots of hands-on exhibits that will teach you more about Milwaukee and the great lakes. Have you ever wondered why Milwaukee discharges sewage into Lake Michigan when it rains? There's a replica of the huge deep tunnel band so you can see just how big it is, and learn what the city is doing to reduce storm water runoff. See how rain barrels and green roofs are making a difference. Learn how Milwaukee makes some of the best drinking water in the world.

Pet stingrays in the touch tank. Follow the changes in sea life as you look into Reiman Aquarium's ten tanks that represent waters from the Great Lakes all the way to the Caribbean Sea.

Sail on Lake Michigan with the S/V Denis Sullivan, if you have time. It's the world's only recreation of a 19th century three masted Great Lakes schooner, used to teach people about maritime history. You can join the crew or sit back and relax. 500 N. Harbor Dr., Milwaukee 53202 (414) 765-9966 www.discoveryworld.org

# 83. HAVE FUN DRESSED LIKE SANTA

Milwaukee is a bicycling city where hardy individuals bike into the snowy days of winter. That being the case, the **Santa Rampage** was born more than a decade past, composed mostly of bike couriers and commuters. Now it has grown into a huge merry event of 500+ riders who dress up and bike through the city. Some out-of-towners even fly in just for the event!

Even if you don't ride a bike, it's fun to dress up and cheer them on along the route, or meet them at one of the destinations for lunch, a drink, and a few photo ops. You never know who might be there.

The Rampage is in late November or early December. Check the Facebook page for Rampage Santa. If you can't join the official tour, you could set up your own ride with friends. It tends to be cold, so be prepared. www.facebook.com/santarampage

If you're more of a running or walking fan, there's the **Santa Hustle**, which is a 5K along the lakefront through Veteran's Park. There are cookies, candy, music, and family fun. You can create your own costume, but you get a Santa hat, beard and sweatshirt with registration. The earlier you register, the lower the fee will be. www.santahustle.com/milwaukee

## 84. VOLUNTEER FOR A WORTHY CAUSE

There are many opportunities to help others here in Milwaukee, and Milwaukeeans tend to be generous. By giving your time to help others, you'll feel better about yourself and your community. You can pick and choose according to your own skill set. If you're not sure where to start, these will get ideas flowing.

**Milwaukee Habitat for Humanity.** If you know how to use tools, this might be for you. Even if you don't have experience, they will work with you as you build homes in Milwaukee neighborhoods. They also have a retail store, called RESTORE, where sales lead to future home projects. You can operate a cash register, greet customers, and answer phones. 3726 N. Booth St., Milwaukee 53212 (414) 562-6100 www.milwaukeehabitat.org

**Victory Garden Initiative.** Their motto is "Move grass. Grow more food". You have probably seen community gardens around Milwaukee created or inspired by this dynamic group. They need help annually with their garden blitz where they install raised garden beds at private homes. If you are a gardener or are just willing to learn, they could benefit from your gift of time. 1845 N. Farwell Ave., Suite 100, Milwaukee 53202 (414) 431-0888. www.victorygardeninitiative.org

**Volunteer Center.** Find opportunities that match your time and interests using the search tool on their website. 2819 W. Highland Blvd., Milwaukee (414) 273-7887 www.volunteermilwaukee.org

**Sharp Literacy.** This is a group dedicated to helping elementary school students build reading, writing and researching skills. The program primarily runs in schools, but volunteers are needed to help with events and to chaperone field trips. 5775 N. Glen Park Rd., Suite 202, Milwaukee 53209 (414) 977-1768 www.sharpliteracy.org

**Milwaukee Rescue Mission.** Dealing with homelessness and poverty is their mission. Every night in Milwaukee 1500 people endure life on the streets of Milwaukee. Even children are affected. They provide meals, clothing, and beds. As a volunteer you could be asked to serve meals, clean classrooms, sort clothing, help with yard work, or staff the nursery. 830 N. 19th St., Milwaukee 53233 (414) 344-2211 www.milmission.org

**Hunger Task Force.** This is an organization that feeds people. They need help sorting food, working special events, stocking at the warehouse, or even working on the farm. 201 S. Hawley Ct., Milwaukee 53214 (414) 238-6473 www.hungertaskforce.org

**Milwaukee County Parks.** Support the parks by volunteering to care for natural areas and trails. Activities involve physical work like planting trees and removing weeds, where you might be using hand tools. If this is for you, contact the volunteer coordinator at (414) 425-8550

**United Way.** Were you a good student? Maybe you'd enjoy working with students by reading to them or helping with homework. 225 W. Vine St., Milwaukee 53212 (414) 263-8100 www.unitedwaymilwaukee.org

**Big Brothers Big Sisters.** Get paired with a young person who could use your friendship. You volunteer a few hours, a couple times per month. This might mean playing video games, going on outings, or just hanging out together. 788 N. Jefferson St., #600, Milwaukee 53202 (414) 258-4778 www.bbbsmilwaukee.org

**Milwaukee Zoo.** If you enjoy working with animals and the public, you can help at the county zoo. There are opportunities to lead tours, educate adults and children at workshops, observe animals, prepare art materials, assist at special events, and much more. Become part of Zoo Pride by completing an application at the website. 10005 W. Bluemound Rd., Milwaukee 53226 (414) 258-2333 www.zoosociety.org

## 85. SMELL THE FLOWERS

For a city our size, we have a lot of green spaces. Some of those are incredibly beautiful with colorful plantings of annuals and perennials. I've already mentioned a good place to see Victorian gardens- **Forest Home Cemetery**. There are three other gardens that are worth a visit.

**Boerner Botanical Gardens**. The rose garden here is an official display garden for the "All-America Rose Selections". The gardens are named for Milwaukee landscape architect, Alfred Boerner, but some of the rose bushes in the garden came from his brother, Eugene, nicknamed "Papa Floribunda" for his work in saving cutting stock from the Nazis during WWII. In spring you'll find the most colorful tulip collection in the county. The peonies are so fragrant when in bloom that you can smell them from across the gardens. There are water features and plenty of flowering shrubs. It's a lovely space where you can take classes, join a garden walk, or just enjoy the scenery. 9400 Boerner Dr., Hales Corners 53130 (414) 525-5600 www.boernerbotanicalgardens.org

**Lynden Sculpture Garden.** This 40-acre sculpture park was once the estate of the late Harry Lynde Bradley, who founded the Allen-Bradley Company. His wife Margaret (Peg) collected art and had the grounds made into an English country park with rolling hills, lake and woodland. 4000 trees were planted here, and the colors look amazing in fall. The fenced flower garden to the side of the former house, which is now the central building, includes annuals perennials along with a few sculptures. 2145 W. Brown Deer Rd., Milwaukee 53217 (414) 446-8794 www.lyndensculpturegarden.org

**Villa Terrace Renaissance Garden.** This is the former residence of former A.O. Smith president, Lloyd Smith and his family. Overlooking Lake Michigan, the garden recreates elements of the 16$^{th}$ century Tuscan landscape. The water stairway flows down past three terraces of flowering crab apples trees. Brides who were married at Villa Terrace donated these dwarf crabapple trees for the Bride's Orchard. Look for culinary and medicinal herbs, potted citrus trees, roses, and 30,000 narcissuses in the spring. The Neptune Gate (above) at the foot of the garden is one of the largest pieces of ironwork crafted in the past century. There's live music at Café Sopre Mare, which adds to the total experience. 2220 N. Terrace Ave., Milwaukee 53202 (414) 271-3656 www.villaterrace.org

If you are more interested in private homes with lovely gardens, sign up for one of the area's garden tours. These are usually held in late summer.

The **Eastside Milwaukee Garden Tour** has a Facebook page at www.facebook.com/EastsideMilwaukeeGardenTour.

The **Riverwest Secret Garden Tour** has a website at www.riverwestsecretgardentour.com.

## 86. GO OUT FOR FRIDAY FISH FRY

Friday night fish fry is a Wisconsin tradition. It all started in Milwaukee when the population was largely Catholic and would eat fish every Friday during Lent. Most restaurants offer fish fry, but there are a few that are unique. For more of a complete list, check the Fox 6 Fish Fry Finder, which includes an interactive map. You can also download the smartphone app called DUN, which lists lots of things, including fish frys by locale. Could it be any easier? www.fox6now.com/community/fish-fry-finder/

**Lakefront Brewery**. Eat in the palm garden with a view of the river. Selections include polish sausage, pulled pork and chicken too, but the perch is raised at the local urban farm Growing Power. If you don't drink alcohol, the maple root beer is a treat. Save room for dessert! Choices include vanilla custard smothered in beer caramel sauce or a chocolate beer cupcake with maple cream frosting and candied bacon. Brewery tours and polka music are also available. 1872 N. Commerce St., Milwaukee 53212 (414) 372-8800 www.lakefrontbrewery.com

**Hubbard Park Lodge.** You might believe you're deep in the north woods when you enter this rustic timber building. Live polka music is played while you eat. Adults can choose potato pancakes or fries with their fish. Kids get fries on their menu. This is affordable and simply so much fun! No reservations are required. Stop by the Beer Garden on the way out of Hubbard Park. 3565 N. Morris Blvd., Milwaukee 53211 (414) 332-4207 www.hubbardlodge.com

**Fish Fry and a Flick.** Enjoy fish fry outdoors at Discovery World while you watch a movie. Films are rated R so this is an adult event. Point beer is featured. Bring a blanket or chair. 500 N. Harbor Dr., Milwaukee 53202 www.pointfishfryandaflick.com

**Tripoli Shrine.** Most people believe it's a mosque, but it is really the meeting place for Shriners, a fraternity based on fun, fellowship, and the Masonic principles of brotherly love, relief and truth. This building (above), an architectural replica of India's Taj Mahal, is on the National Register of Historic Places. For the fish fry, tables are set in the gorgeous rotunda where light streams onto the tiled mosaic floor. Real gold decorates the walls. Be sure to take the stairs up to the second floor while you wait for your food, so you can look down on the first floor. Everything on the menu is good, but if you can't decide, go for the combo plate where you get several kinds of fish, coleslaw, rye bread, and a potato pancake you can top with applesauce and real maple syrup. 3000 W. Wisconsin Ave., Milwaukee 53208 (414) 933-4700 www.tripolishrinecenter.com

**Kegel's Inn.** It's the most authentic German beer hall and restaurant in the area, with fast service and German recipes. Take a good look around the building noting the stained glass windows and polished wooden bar. Every piece of fish is individually battered and fried. The cod is a favorite, but it wouldn't be complete without all the fixings like potato pancakes cooked to perfection. Good selection of German beers. 5901 W. National Ave., Milwaukee 53214 (414) 257-9999 www.kegelsinn.com

**County Clare.** Milwaukee's only Irish inn and pub, where you can dine outdoors in summer and hear live polka music, while you drink your stout. You can eat your fish with malt vinegar, just like they do in Ireland! If you have a mixed crowd for dinner, they also have vegetarian and gluten free options. 1234 N. Astor St., Milwaukee 53202 (414) 272-5273 www.countyclare-inn.com

## 87. RIDE THE POLKA ESCALATOR

The polka escalator is an amazing contraption housed inside the Wisconsin Center. You have to visit when the center is open (between 9-5) and there aren't any private functions. Sometimes that can be a bit challenging, but I guarantee it will be worth the effort. The escalator is nearest the Hilton walkway by 6th and Wisconsin, on the 2nd to 3rd floor. When you arrive, find the button that says, "Push to Play Polka". What you hear next might startle you, as it is quite loud. The announcer tells you the polka and then proceeds to play it. Photos of a polka party line the wall as you ascend.

While you're inside the center, walk around and notice the tall palm trees, interesting prose written on walls, and other artwork. It's a beautiful space filled with the $1.2 million Burke family art collection. Be sure to say hi to the security guard on the way out, near the 4th street door. Is he real? There's more artwork out on the sidewalk, including old callboxes and fire hydrants, lion heads, and a set of stairs.

Wisconsin Center, 400 W. Wisconsin Ave., Milwaukee 53203. www.wisconsincenter.org

## 88. TRY AN OUTRAGEOUS BLOODY MARY

Whenever there is a national competition for Bloody Marys, Milwaukee always comes out a winner. I'm not sure how it all happened, but there has been a constant series of one-upmanship when it comes to creating the garnish at our local bars. Though it should be more about taste, it's all about making a meal of the drink. They are outrageous and unique at every bar you visit. It's impossible to say where the best drink is because everyone likes something different, but here are three places you can't go wrong. You can always order a non-alcoholic version if you prefer not to drink. It's a great way to start out the weekend, but they are actually available any time.

**Sobelman's Pub & Grill.** If you have a large group, you can order a pitcher with a complete chicken attached. 1900 W. St. Paul Ave., Milwaukee 53233 (414) 931-1919 www.milwaukeesbestburgers.com

**Wicked Hop.** Their house recipe includes a garnish of shrimp, beef stick, dill pickle, mozzarella whips, a mushroom and an olive. They have a lovely covered patio that welcomes dogs. 345 N. Broadway, Milwaukee 53202 (414) 223-0345 www.thewickedhop.com

**AJ Bombers.** No mixes here. Everything from scratch and a slice of Muenster burger wrapped in bacon. Peanut bombers bring peanuts to your table while you wait. 1247 N. Water St., Milwaukee 53202 (414) 221-9999 www.ajbombers.com

## 89. WATCH A MOVIE OUTDOORS

Pack up the car with a blanket, some chairs, and maybe a warm jacket for one of Milwaukee Park's FREE outdoor movie nights. Food trucks are usually available. You'll want to arrive early for the best seating. Shows start at dusk. There are a couple of venues- some are more family friendly than others.

**Milwaukee County Parks** has movies in Veteran's Park, Humboldt Park, and LaFollette Park. The Family Flicks schedule is posted in early summer. www.milwaukee.gov and search for family flicks.

**Point Fish Fry and a Flick.** Held outdoors at Discovery World, these are adult movies (rated R). Point Brewery beer and Bartolotta's fish fry are available for purchase. 500 N. Harbor Dr., Milwaukee 53202 www.pointfishfryandaflick.com

**Bike-in Movie Nights.** Under the Holton Street Bridge, you'll see a series of movies during summer hosted by the Milwaukee Bike Community. Follow the Milwaukee Bike-In Movie Series on Facebook.

# 90. GO TO AN OUTDOOR CONCERT OR PLAY

Not only is Milwaukee the "City of Festivals", we have free concerts outdoors nearly every day from early June until late August. The county parks will put out a schedule in late spring that covers the major venues, but each municipality also has concerts. Here are the major players:

**Humboldt Park Chill on the Hill.** Tuesdays at 6:00. 3000 S. Howell Ave, Milwaukee

**Washington Park Wednesdays at the Shell.** Wednesdays at 6:00. 1859 N. 40th St., Milwaukee

**Pere Marquette Park River Rhythms.** Wednesdays at 6:30. 900 N. Plankinton Ave., Milwaukee

**Cathedral Square Jazz in the Park.** Thursdays. Happy hour 5-6. Music at 6:00. 520 E. Wells St., Milwaukee

**Lake Park Musical Mondays.** Mondays at 6:30. 2975 N. Lake Park Rd., Milwaukee

**Kadish Park.** Host to Optimist Theatre's Shakespeare in the Park (www.optimisttheatre.org) and the Skyline Music Series. Tuesday. 5:30-8:30 308 E. Lloyd St., Milwaukee 53212

**Colectivo.** Florentine Opera and Musica del Lago Latin Performance Series play at the Lakefront Colectivo on Thursdays. Riverwest and Bay View cafes have the opera on Wednesdays.

**Catalano Square.** Thursdays at 6:30. 320 E. Menomonee St., Milwaukee 53202 www.musicinthesquare.org

## 91. DANCE LIKE NO ONE IS WATCHING

Have you ever wanted to learn to dance? It's fun and great exercise! Take some lessons or just hit the dance floor. Here are a variety of options, but the list is not all-inclusive. Some clubs have a cover charge.

Radio personality Julie Davidson danced with **Astor Street Studios** CJ (above) at the charitable Dancing with our Stars event, after just a few practice sessions. It's amazing what you can learn when you're motivated. At Astor Studios you can take a few lessons in ballroom, salsa, or even belly dance before you hit the dance club floor. 1228 N. Astor St., Milwaukee (414) 208-9021 www.astorstreetdance.com

**Ko-Thi Dance Company.** Learn how to do a variety of African dances. Drop-ins welcome. Pay per class. UWM Peck School of the Arts, Mitchell Hall Rm 256 3203 N. Downer Ave., Milwaukee 53211 (414) 273-0676 www.ko-thi.org

**Danceworks.** Both dance and fitness classes for all skill levels. Ballet, ballroom, hip-hop, jazz, tap, and even classes for people over age 50. 1661 N. Water St., Milwaukee 53202 (414) 277-8480 www.danceworksmke.org

**Folk Dancing.** If you're more inclined to try folk dancing, you can find something nearly every night at different spaces around the city. We have Scottish country dancing, Israeli dancing, international folk dancing, and contra dancing. Beginners are usually welcome. The best source to find the venues is a website called www.balkanmusic.com.

**Hot Water Nightclub/Wherehouse.** A converted warehouse with two dance clubs, you might have to look a bit to find the entrances. A different theme every night. They also offer dance instruction. You'll find tango, rock n roll, swing, salsa, and top 40. This is a high-energy place where you won't need a table because everyone is on the dance floor. Check the website for hours and events. 818 S. Water St., Milwaukee 53204 (414) 383-7593 www.hotwatermilwaukee.com

**Kochanski's Concertina Beer Hall.** Drop in on a Wednesday night for polka dancing starting at 7 PM. They also offer other genres during the weekends. This is a fun place with two stages so you'll end up in the front of the show at some point when they do dueling stages. Polish and German beers on tap with a new beer garden. 1920 S. 37th St., Milwaukee 53215 (414) 837-6552 www.beer-hall.com

**Victor's Cocktail Lounge & Restaurant.** Daily drink specials. Dance party starts at 9 PM in the Las Vegas style nightclub. Music from the 60s to today's hits. They also have a dinner menu. 1230 N. Van Buren St., Milwaukee 53202 www.victorsnightclub.com

**La Cage.** The largest gay (everyone welcome) dance and entertainment complex in Wisconsin. You'll find multiple floors, a dance cage, female impersonators, and live DJs. 801 S. 2nd St., Milwaukee 53204 (414) 383-8330 www.lacage.mke.com

**Studio Lounge.** Known for salsa lessons, art on the walls, and great drinks. 2246 S. Kinnickinnic Ave., Milwaukee 53207 (414) 489-7474 www.studioloungemke.com

**Mad Planet.** Friday night retro dance parties every week. Themed shows and a variety of live entertainment. 533 E. Center St., Milwaukee 53212 www.mad-planet.net

## 92. TRY SOMETHING AT A FOOD TRUCK

Milwaukee's food trucks are bringing lunch and dinner to you at events all over the city. To find out where they are every day, go to the tracking website www.roaminghunger.com/mke or follow them at Tap Milwaukee on twitter where you can subscribe to Milwaukee Food Trucks. At the Roaming Hunger you can read about each truck and see menus. If you're the kind of person who wants to do them all, download the Milwaukee DUN app to your smartphone and do the entire list of food trucks.

Generally you'll find trucks at outdoor concerts like Chill on the Hill, River Rhythms, Westown Farmer's Market, East Side Green Market, and East Town Farmer's Market. During warmer months on a Tuesday, you can have lunch in Schlitz Park when 15 trucks line up across from Manpower Headquarters. Food Truck Thursday brings them to the Milwaukee County Courthouse from 11-2.

There are a wide variety of foods; sandwiches, bubble tea, grilled cheese, BBQ, chicken with special sauces, cold pressed juice, tacos, nachos, Belgian style fries, pizza and more. All of them have a special talent and at least one has national recognition. Forbes and GQ magazines recognized STREET-ZA in lists of fantastic food trucks. They make delicious pizza by the slice. Find one and give it a try!

## 93. LOOK AT THE LAKE THROUGH THE WINDOWS OF THE CALATRAVA

When trying to impress out-of-town guests, the first place most locals come is the **Milwaukee Art Museum**. This gorgeous building is the architectural landmark in the city! It has even been featured in movies like *Transformers* and *Bridesmaids*. The portion with the wings that open is called the Quadracci Pavilion, which was designed by Santiago Calatrava.

Of course, as one would expect, the building contains a huge collection of impressive art with changing exhibits. There's also a gift shop featuring both local and artisan items. There's a special place to make your own art with kids- the Kohl's Education Center. You can pick up an art pack and do activities throughout the museum. Adults can enjoy lectures, tours, and take classes.

If you want to meet a friend for coffee, sit in the café or out on the patio with a view of the lake. For a larger meal, go down to the restaurant where the menu changes with the featured exhibition. You won't need to pay admission for the café or the restaurant. At least one day per month, admission is free (first Thursday sponsored by Target). Kids age 12 and under are always free. Teachers K-12 also receive free admission with an ID card. 700 N. Art Museum Dr., Milwaukee 53202 (414) 224-3200 www.mam.org

## 94. RIDE THE PEDAL TAVERN

What could be more fun than meeting friends at a bar? How about pedaling yourselves around the city as you enjoy a frosty beverage? The **Milwaukee Pedal Tavern** is a 16-person bicycle powered party on wheels.

You don't need to have 15 of your own friends; you can sign up for a public pub-crawl and make some new friends for about $25. There is a driver who knows the area and will steer the group. Tour the Third Ward and Walker's Point with stops at 3-5 bars. You decide how much you want to drink, as the cost of drinks is not included in the price. The bars that participate do run drink specials, though. You are allowed to bring up to three cans of beer per person (BYOB), if you prefer. You can also book it for your own group and do a progressive pub-crawl or dinner tour.

Tours start at Steny's Tavern and are available from 10 am-10:30 pm. Have a friend unable to pedal? No problem. There are three seats at the back with no pedals. 2nd at National. Book online or call to make a reservation. (414) 405-6682 www.pedaltavern.com

## 95. LOOK FOR PUBLIC ART

It goes by different names- yard art, public art, murals, or even graffiti. These are spaces that are made more interesting by their appearance. Their very existence seems to keep vandals at bay, so they are encouraged and add something to the Milwaukee landscape. Some of them pop up overnight. Groups using art funds commission others. Not only are there paintings, you might see empty lots transformed into pocket parks with flowerbeds or garden patches.

Google "**Milwaukee Mural Map**" and you'll find a map with about 40 murals, which include photos if you click on the cameras. If you don't have access, here are some I think are worth a look.

Reynaldo Hernandez, a local artist, painted the mural above on the side of **Esperanza Unida International Building**. Look closely and you'll see what a big job it was to paint individual panels that were hung separately to make the huge piece of artwork. He did a project with students during summer 2014 in Silver City neighborhood at 35th & National, under the bridge. The rooftop sheep on a nearby building inspired the design. 611 W. National Ave., Milwaukee 53204.

There's a self guided **Hispanic Heritage Tour** that includes murals by Reynaldo and other artists. Stop in at the United Community Center to learn more about Latinos in Milwaukee and download the mural walk at http://www.unitedcc.org/Self_Guided_UCC_Tour.pdf.

Drive down Martin Luther King Dr. and you'll see a variety of African American themed murals, starting with MLK Jr. Elementary School at 3rd St. Then additional murals at Clinton & Bernice Rose Senior Center, All

Makes Radiator Repair, and Victory over Violence Park.

**Milwaukee Monster Mural**, is at 224-1st. St. There are additional colorful murals at Richardson & 27th; 22nd at National; and on the side of Anodyne Coffee at 3rd at Bruce St.

There are some **pop-up parks** featuring art work at 29th & Burnham; Madison Garden at 32nd & Madison; and across from Amaranth Bakery at 3327 W. Lisbon. It's great to see empty lots turn into something both beautiful and useful.

Sometimes residents decide to decorate in a unique way. You can see a yard at Cherry & 33rd that has everything including the Hamburglar. Go to 2659 N. Humboldt in Riverwest to see a buried half car. There's a boat house at 3128 Cambridge.

If sculpture is more your thing, you must see **Cass Street Park**, 1647 N. Cass St. This was a revitalization effort, which included colorful sculptures of a cat, dragon, and whimsical bird done by local artist Marina Lee. She also has more public art at a pocket park on Martin Luther King Dr. and at Snail's Crossing, 3500 N. Bremen. www.marinalee.com

**Catalano Square-** This small city park, which is more of a triangle, contains a very interesting sculpture that looks more like a cage. It's a compilation of all the historic pieces and parts that came out of the warehouses in the area. It's meant to be walked through. 320 E. Menomonee St., Milwaukee 53202

**The Artery** is a rail to trail project that connects Harambee and Riverwest neighborhoods, which is focused on showing off local artwork. Performances take place during the summer. All visitors may enter the trail from 4 locations: on N. Richards just north of Keefe Ave., at either end of the footbridge above Capitol Dr. near N. 3rd St., or where E. Abert Pl. meets the trail, just west of the intersection with N. 1st St. www.creationaltrails.com

# 96. SEE A FRANK LLOYD WRIGHT BUILDING

Frank Lloyd Wright's influence is seen in a few buildings in Milwaukee. Unfortunately he died before he was able to see the **Annunciation Greek Orthodox Church** (above) completed. The floor plan is a Greek cross, with a domed Byzantine roof inspired by the Hagia Sophia in Turkey. The best way to see the church is to come for a Sunday liturgy and experience the acoustics. Tours are available for groups of 15 or more on Tuesday and Fridays between 11-2. 9400 W. Congress St., Milwaukee 53225 (414) 461-9400 www.annunciationwi.org

This beautiful church is definitely the highlight but there are **American System-Built Homes** as well. He was asked to design a group of homes on West Burnham. Simple and small, they were affordable which was key in the early 1900s. Six were built in a row, and though they have been altered, you can definitely recognize his architectural style. Tour dates are listed on the website, but you can drive by and take a look any time. Interior tours of the Model B1 at 2714 W. Burnham are led by docents at a cost of $10 per adult, and no reservations are necessary. They will point out interesting details you might otherwise miss. It has been completely restored. You'll find functional built-in cabinets and closets, beautiful wood throughout, lots of windows, a sleeping porch, and a lovely brick fireplace. www.wrightinmilwaukee.org

## 97. TASTE SOME HOT FRIED CHEESE CURDS

Nothing says Dairy State like fresh squeaky cheese curds, but we like them fried too. There's really nothing healthy about them. They just taste good. Lots of bars and restaurants in Milwaukee have a version of them. You can check www.yelp.com for suggestions, or here are a few places with some good ones.

**Motor Bar & Restaurant.** This restaurant at the Harley Davidson museum serves up burgers and cheese. 401 W. Canal St., Milwaukee 53201 (414) 287-2778 www.motorrestaurant.com

**AJ Bombers.** This place has been featured on Food Wars on Food Network and is known for great burgers and the peanutty interior. 1247 N. Water St., Milwaukee 53202 (414) 221-9999 www.ajbombers.com

**Milwaukee Brat House.** Get your cheese curds with beer and brats here. 1013 N. Old World 3rd St., Milwaukee 53203 (414) 273-8709 www.milwaukeebrathouse.com

**Major Goolsby's**. Come as you are, whether it's all dressed up from the theater or casual. Lots of televisions in this sports bar convenient to downtown sporting events. 340 W. Kilbourn Ave., Milwaukee 53203 www.majorgoolsbys.com

## 98. SEE THE HOLIDAY DISPLAYS

The lights of Christmas are a welcome sight when temperatures are frigid and we spend hours in darkness. Like so many things Milwaukee does, we make a big party out of seeing holiday decorations.

**Holiday Lights Festival.** This runs from mid-November through just after Christmas. You can take the Jingle Bus from Grand Avenue Mall for $1. Buy tickets from Center Court- 275 W. Wisconsin Avenue. Be sure to see the Christmas Bears and grab a free cookie inside before you get onboard. It's a narrated city tour where you'll see the most decorated scenes and plenty of downtown landmarks.

Drink cocoa with the Clauses at Cathedral Square Park one special weekend or drop off a note to Santa's mailbox all season long. You can get a keepsake photo, hear holiday music, and play reindeer games. www.milwaukeedowntown.com/about-us/special-events/milwaukee-holiday-lights-festival

**BMO Harris Bank** 150 Stuffed Steiff animals are put into a new holiday setting every year in the bank lobby. This runs from early December into early January. It's free and open to the public. 770 N. Water St., Milwaukee 53202.

**Candy Cane Lane**. This is outside of the city, but that doesn't stop droves of cars from heading out to see it. A neighborhood that really puts out the lights, you can read more at their website. It all began in 1984 when a neighborhood wanted to raise funds for childhood cancer. Now 300 homes participate and $100,000 is raised from donations. 96th St. to 92nd St., Montana Ave. to Oklahoma Ave in West Allis. This runs the day after Thanksgiving until a couple days after Christmas. Bring your own cocoa. www.candycanelanewi.com

## 99. OOH AND AAHH AT LAKEFRONT FIREWORKS

Most cities get to see fireworks just once a year. We're spoiled here, as there are fireworks shows nearly every weekend during the summer festival season. You can go to the fireworks website and select Milwaukee as the city http://fireworksinwisconsin.com/by-city/milwaukee-wisconsin/ for a complete listing of events where fireworks will be held. Then go stake out a place near Discovery World or Veterans Park for the best seats in town.

## 100. WATCH REALLY FAST CARS AT THE MILWAUKEE MILE

The Milwaukee Mile is a one-mile long oval racetrack at Wisconsin State Fair Park with plenty of grandstand and bleacher seating. This is the oldest operating motor speedway in the world! The first automobile race was held here in 1903. Most people don't know that the infield was the home of the NFL's Green Bay Packers from 1934-1953. Now it's used for at least one race a year, and is also home to the Rusty Wallace Racing Experience.

Indyfest comes in mid-August, right after the state fair. You can hear the hum of Indy cars doing laps from miles away. Be sure to wear earplugs if you plan to attend. In addition to the races, there's a family fun zone where rides are free with admission to Indyfest. You'll find live music, a beer garden, concessions, and opportunities to get autographs in the fan village. 7722 W. Greenfield, West Allis 53214 www.milwaukeemile.com

If you're ready for a more hands-on approach to racing, get on board with the Rusty Wallace Racing Experience where you can drive a racecar or ride along with a driver. It comes to Milwaukee several times a year, but isn't here permanently. www.racewithrusty.com

For a full listing of events at the Milwaukee Mile, go to the Wisconsin State Fair website. http://wistatefair.com/wsfp/milwaukee-mile-speedway-and-peck-media-center/

## 101. GET TO KNOW YOUR COLLEGES

People come from all over the globe to attend our colleges, but most locals have rarely been, unless they studied here. Pick a campus and get to know more about programs offered, the students, or a topic that interests you. Here is just a little information to pique your interest. Talk to some students and you'll likely discover even more. You could invite students to your family Thanksgiving or Christmas celebrations, if you're feeling generous.

**Milwaukee School Of Engineering** has a fitness center that offers public memberships, yoga classes, and even an ice rink (shown in the photo above). They also offer a program for book lovers called "Great Books Dinner and Discussion" at the Alumni Partnership Center. It's a monthly event to discuss books and enjoy a themed gourmet dinner. Check the events page for more information. www.msoe.edu

**University Wisconsin- Milwaukee** houses the fantastic American Geographical Society Map Collection which includes more than one million items- maps, atlases, books, photographs, and images. You can often stop by the library to see an exhibit, or come for an author talk. Schedule a visit to 2311 E. Hartford Ave., which is the third floor of the Golda Meir Library. (414) 229-6282 www.uwm.edu/libraries/agsl/visit/.

The UWM Union Theatre shows a number of films, and many are free. All programs are open to the public. You will see independent films that premiered at the Sundance Film Festival, experimental films, historically significant films, and much more. To find out what is playing, check out the calendar link at www.aux.uwm.edu/union/union_theatre/

The Peck School of Arts has a number of fine arts programs that bring events to the public. Check the calendar to find concerts featuring the world-renowned string quartet, faculty artists, jazz, guitarists, and other student ensembles. It's an impressive line-up and many performances are free. http://psoacal.uwm.edu/?post_type=tribe_events

UWM's new School of Freshwater Sciences is the only graduate school in the nation dedicated to the study of fresh water. Anyone can attend their Anchor Watch seminars. Check the events page to see what fascinating speakers and topics are coming. 600 E. Greenfield Ave., Milwaukee www.glwi.uwm.edu/features/events/anchor.php

**Marquette University** has a variety of special collections, including the J.R.R. Tolkien original manuscripts, which are on display through 2015. Find out more about the Raynor Library collections and showings at the university website. www.marquette.edu. There's a full service dental clinic at the School of Dentistry, which is open to the public ages 13 and older. www.marquette.edu/dentistry/patients/PatientsIndex.shtml. The Speech and Hearing Clinic offer hearing tests and speech therapy for a fee. www.marquette.edu/speech-pathology-audiology/clinic.shtml

**Milwaukee Area Technical College's** culinary program has turned out a number of chefs who currently work at local restaurants. You can eat at the campus restaurant, called "Cuisine", and taste the work of current students. Check the website for mealtimes being offered along with a seasonal menu. Then schedule your lunch via the website. Located in room M102 in the main building on the downtown campus. 700 W. State St., Milwaukee 53233 www.matc.edu/cuisine/

Stop in for bakery and coffee made by MATC students. Open Monday through Thursday, 11:15-1:45, at the 6th Street Bakery on the downtown campus, main building, room 175A.

Hair, nail, and spa services are offered to men and women in the main building on the first floor. www.matc.edu/communityresources/hair.cfm

Students at the Health Sciences Building offer dental cleanings and X-rays during the school year. 700 W. Highland Ave., Room H115. (414) 297-6573. www.matc.edu/communityresources/dental.cfm

**Cardinal Stritch University** has the Kendall lecture series featuring speakers of national prominence. There is also a performing arts program, which offers four productions a year, from musicals to classics. If you're in need of a speaker for an event, they have an extensive list of speakers and topics. For more information check their community page. www.stritch.edu/community/

**Alverno College** brings in talented performers monthly. These events are generally open to the public. They host the free Global Union Music Festival each fall at Humboldt Park. You can check out the Alverno Presents schedule at www.alvernopresents.alverno.edu/shows/ or find additional events on the calendar at www.alverno.edu.

# Conclusion

By the time you get to the end of this book, I hope you've found something to love about Milwaukee. It's a city challenged with budget problems, politics, and unemployment, just like many other places. If you've had time to complete all the adventures, you definitely know more about Milwaukee and its culture now. You've likely met some new people and learned a few things you didn't know before.

I have one more suggestion for you. Consider it extra credit. It's a tough job holding any position in county or city government. Why not take a minute to send a note to a local official of your choice to let them know what you love about this city. Give them your support and some positive encouragement. It really takes a village to keep this city beautiful, active, historic, and wonderful.

For the city of Milwaukee directory www.city.milwaukee.gov or mail to City Hall, 200 E. Wells St., Room 201, Milwaukee WI, 53202

For the county of Milwaukee directory www.county.milwaukee.gov or mail to Milwaukee County Courthouse, 901 N. 9th St., Room 306, Milwaukee WI 53233

If you've enjoyed the book, you can recommend it to others by leaving a review at www.amazon.com or www.goodreads.com. If you have suggestions for future revisions, you can drop me a line at alibarbara1@gmail.com. I enjoy hearing from readers!

## SUGGESTED ITINERARIES
(Bucket list numbers follow the experience.)

### Brady Street Neighborhood
Brunch at Trocadero-20
Swing Park-5
Lakefront Brewery Tour-6
Climb to the top of Kilbourn Reservoir Park for the view-47
Cass Street Park-95
Sciortino's Bakery-60
Glorioso's Italian Market-46
Rochambo Coffee & Tea House-12

### Washington Heights
Art & Soul art gallery- 29
Take your dog to doggie dining at Nourri- 67
Blow some glass at Square One Art Glass-30
Buy a gift at Barcelona-80
Drink some quality coffee at Valentine Coffee-19
Meritage for a vegetarian dinner-75

### Historic Third Ward
Bloody Mary at Wicked Hop-88
Pick up chocolate at Red Elephant-42
Bakery at Holey Moley-60
Photo Walk or Food Tour-18
Harley Davidson Museum-11
Milwaukee Pedal Tavern-94
FORE! Golf simulator-33

### Walker's Point
Braise green rooftop dining-27
Stone Creek Coffee-19
88Nine Radio Milwaukee live show-45
Indulgence Chocolatiers chocolate pairing bar-42
Ride the chili pepper at La Perla-40
Brewery Tour at Milwaukee Brewing Co. or Brenner Brewing Co.-6
Great Lakes and Central Standard Distillery tours-6
Purple Door Ice Cream-7
Comedy Sportz-77
Cheese tour at Clock Shadow Creamery-37
Green roof at Clock Tower Shadow building-27
CORE/El Centro farmer's market on rooftop-2

Zenzen aerial yoga-62
Hometown Established for a local gift-80
Brunch at Smyth-20
Staycation at the Iron Horse Hotel-54
Dance at La Cage-91

## Bay View
Coffee at Anodyne or Colectivo -19
Anodyne Coffee Roasting Co. & mural-19/95
Humboldt Park beer garden-71
Hamburger Mary Drag Queen Show-77
Buy a hat at the Brass Rooster-80
Taste chocolate at Chocobella-42
Buy a gift at Sparrow Collective-80
Go bowling at Bay View Bowl-1
Have ice cream drinks at At Random or soy ice cream at Babe's-7
Share pie at Honeypie-60

## Lakefront Fun
Northpoint Custard-7
Take a dip at Bradford Beach-8
Coffee at Colectivo at the Lake-19
Veteran's Park stand up paddleboard-51
Fly a kite at Veteran's Park-64
Segway tour or bike along the lakefront path-48
Discovery World-82
Art Museum-93
War Memorial-53

## Free Activities
Newaukee Night Market-2
Swing under Holton Street Bridge-5
Miller Brewery Tour-7
Swim in Lake Michigan-11
Caterpillar Heritage Museum-10
Learn to unicycle-16
Self guided walking tour-18
Forest Home Cemetery-21
St. Joan of Arc Chapel-23
Basilica of St. Josaphat-24
Watch a sunrise-26
Visit UWM's art galleries-29
Visit the Domes on a Monday if you're a Milwaukee resident-32

Tour the library's green roof-27
Go to the Newsroom-39
Do the radio show at 88Nine-45
Climb to the top of Kilbourn Reservoir Park-47
Have a picnic-52
See the War memorial-53
Attend an event at Boswell Book Co.-61
Take a free yoga class at Bayshore Mall during summer-62
Go geocaching- 63
Fly a kite- 85
Take a hike- 72
Do Atwater stairs- 78
See fall colors at Holy Hill- 100
Ride the Polka Escalator- 87
See an outdoor movie- 89
Go to a concert in the parks- 90
Go inside the Milwaukee Art Museum to see the wings-93
See some outdoor art- 95
Go to the holiday displays at Cathedral Square-98
Watch the fireworks from Lakeshore State Park during Summerfest-129

## Rainy Day
Any museum on the list-10
Swing Park-5
Cheese tour-37
Milwaukee Historical Society-15
Brewery /Distillery Tour-6
Art Gallery Tour-29
Bowling-1
Northpoint Lighthouse-9
FORE! Golf-33
Growing Power tour-31
Domes-32
Casino-41
Pabst Mansion tour-44

## My Mother-in-Law is in Town
Grohmann Museum rooftop garden-17
Boerner Botanical Garden-85
Pfister Blu Afternoon Tea-12
Purple Door Ice Cream-7
Basilica of St. Josaphat-24
Put her up in a Boutique Hotel-54

Indulgence chocolate pairing with cheese-42
Ride the trolley-65
Tour Forest Home Cemetery-21
Bookstore event-61
Boat tour-43
Angelo's Piano Bar-34
Untapped Tour of Milwaukee-18

## Bachelor Party/Guys Day Out
Milwaukee Blacksmith session-30
Brewery or Distillery Tour-6
Pedal Tavern-94
Hockey, Admirals, or Brew City Bruisers game-14
Foot Golf outing-33
Rock Climbing at Turner Hall-16
Bowling-1
Comedy Sportz-77

## Bachelorette Party/Girls Day Out
Spa Day-73
Square One Art Glass or Splash party-30
Tea at Schuster Mansion-12
The Safe House-4
Cooking Class-70
Murder Mystery Dinner-77
Themed dance night at Hot Water/Wherehouse-91
Aerial Yoga at ZenZen-62
Lucille's Piano Bar-34

## Date Night
Go bowling- 1
See a live theater show- 4
Play ping pong- 16
Take a Milwaukee Food Tour- 18
Eat at Tochi or Braise where they have growing roofs- 27
Nite-glow golf outing- 46
See a film at a film festival- 48
Boat tour from the river- 58
Have a staycation- 72
Take a horse & carriage ride- 72
Find a new ethnic restaurant- 55
Go out for fish fry- 113
Dance- 119

## Total Kids' Day
Betty Brinn-10
Ride the Polka Escalator-87
Farmer's Market-2
The Domes-32
Fly a kite-64
Have a picnic-52
Cream City Rickshaw ride-58
Urban Ecology Center-25, 27,59
Zoo-22
Classy Girl Cupcakes-60
Outdoor movie-89
Climb North Point Lighthouse stairs-9
Organ Piper Pizza-34
Kadish Park Concert-90
Photo with the Bronze Fonz and walk riverwalk-79

## Summer for Outdoor Lovers
Hike a park-72
Beer Garden-71
Lynden Sculpture Garden-85
Braise rooftop garden-27
Milwaukee Geocaching Tour-63
UWM telescope at night on the roof-74
Hit the beach-8
Kayak the rivers-69
Paddleboard at Veteran's Park-51
Lakefront biking-48
Outdoor yoga-62
Movie in a park-89
Outdoor concert-90
Grohmann roof top garden-17
Milwaukee County Zoo-22
Walking tour-18
Boat tour-43
Oak Leaf Trail passport-49
Sailing lesson-16
Waterpark-81
Boerner Botanical Garden-85

## Smart Phone Apps you might find helpful:

**OnMilwaukee**- contains articles, blogs and podcasts you might find at their regular website. A great reference for what's happening in town.

**Yelp**- reviews and helpful advice for finding any building in any city. These tend to be locals who write the reviews. Use the search tool to find restaurants, grocers, parks, anything!

**Tripadvisor**- traveler reviews by people who visit hotels, restaurants, and attractions. These tend to be worldwide reviewers.

**Google Maps**- helps you find your way walking, bicycling, by bus, or driving.

**Groupon**- find coupons and deals for Milwaukee area businesses.

**Living Social**- Similar to Groupon with deals

**Oh Ranger, Park Finder**- Uses the phone's GPS to find nearby parks. Great when you need to stretch your legs. Gives good descriptions of the parks so you know if there's a playground and bathrooms.

**Market Finder.** Uses GPS to find nearby farmers markets. You can click on the map destinations for information about address, date, time, and products.

**DUN.** A Milwaukee app featuring a variety of lists that you can check off. Look for biking, art galleries, restaurants, fish frys, food trucks, and so much more. This could become your favorite app for where to go.

**SpotHero Parking**- put in your local destination and it provides the address and cost for parking nearby

**Milwaukee Zoo**- has tools to help you plan your visit and a map you can use to navigate your way through the grounds.

**WI State Fair**- daily schedule of events, discounts, and location information

**Milwaukee Bikes**- incredibly helpful for newer cyclists to the city. It gives routes depending on how you ride and what you want to see. It even includes the Oak Leaf Discovery Tour.

**River Keeper Swim Guide**- Uses your GPS to find nearby beaches and lets you know the water quality.

**Milwaukee Admirals**- scores, news, and the schedule for fans

**Milwaukee Journal Sentinel**- the latest local news

**Milwaukee Soldier's Home**- free walking tour of the Milwaukee Soldiers Home so you can learn more about this historic landmark

**Summerfest**- everything you need to know about schedule and stage line-up. Helps you navigate once you're at the park. Information about food and drinks.

**MPM Exhibit Guide**- handy maps and information about exhibits

**Festa MKE-** Festa Italiana information about entertainment, parking, and vendors.

## ABOUT THE AUTHOR

Barbara Ali is a native of Illinois, but spent the bulk of her adult life
traveling the world as she served a career with the US Air Force. She is an
avid photographer, world traveler, adventurer, and mom. She and her
husband, Abdulhamid, live in Milwaukee, Wisconsin, where they have a
"yours, mine, and ours" family of six children.

Made in the USA
Columbia, SC
05 January 2019